Cross-Border Migration

MIZORAM

Cross-Border Migration
MIZORAM

Edited by: Sangkima

Maulana Abul kalam Azad Institute of Asian Studies

SHIPRA

Published on behalf of Maulana Abul Kalam Azad Institute of Asian Studies, Kolkata. Views expressed are those of the contributors and do not reflect the position of the Institute.

Rs. 795

ISBN: 978-8175-4117-53

2024, Reprint
(First Published in India in 2004)

Cross-Border Migration – Mizoram

Published by:
SHIPRA PUBLICATIONS
LG 18-19, Pankaj Central Market
I.P. Ext., Patparganj, Delhi 110092
91 11 47322068; 9650028065, 9810522367
info@shiprapublication.com
www.shiprapublication.com

Contents

1

Introduction

Sangkima

One significant issue now encircling very country in the world today is immigration. It is said that until the first two post-war decades, immigration was perhaps not an issue of dispute between nations mainly because the economic expansion in Europe and other parts of the globe, especially after World War-II, demanded and needed more labour force. For this outlying reason, people of different backgrounds moved from one country to another without any hindrance or restrictions. But the situation has dramatically changed since the last two decades or so. Now, immigration on a large scale has resulted in great ethnic explosions amongst ethnic communities in a country. Therefore, ethnic problem is rampant everywhere in the world.

In this regard, a very unhealthy climate is emerging in Europe. For the first time in postwar Europe, many far Right political

> parties are in the offing and these parties are gaining alarming political momentum. In recent local elections all over Europe these parties have won a significant number of seats and harp on one nation, one culture and even one common language. Their leaders say that if elected to power in their countries they would shut the doors to immigrants and send them back to their countries of origin. If this is the emerging trend the future of Europe hangs in balance and it is likely that sooner or later there will be a repetition of what Hitler did to the Jews more than half a century ago.

Like other places in the world, India's problem with illegal immigrants is vulnerable. Bounded by international borders on all sides, India is bound to have infiltration problems. In this matter, the western part of the country with international borders all along the States of Rajasthan and Gujarat needs serious consideration. North India is also bound by the same problem. This region has been offering a fertile land for foreign intruders since the time of Alexander's invasion of India in B.C. 326. Since the coming of the Arabs in Sindh in the early twelfth century A.D. this region has been frequented by infiltrators. As a result, the problems being faced by north India are complexed and complicated more than those of any other part of the country.

The issue of illegal immigrants has also encompassed the whole North-East India. In one sense, the problem of North-East India is possibly worse and more complicated than other parts of the country because different ethnic races could easily enter any part of this region. Bounded by four international borders this tract has provided an easy access to various foreign elements. Consequent upon this, the immigrant problem of this area is acute. To make the problem more complicated, every political party is trying to make capital out of it. It is needless to say that the problem of illegal movements of people in North-East India is said to have influenced, to a great extent, the rise of insurgencies in the region. Whatever may be the state of politics in the North-East India the fact is that those who are responsible for the North-East States must admit that the problems facing this region are getting more complexed and complicated day in and day out.

With this background in view, it may be pointed out that the seminar on "Cross-Border Movements of People Into Mizoram" sponsored by Maulan Abul Kalam Azad Institute of Asian Studies (MAKAIAS) held on 25th April, 2002 at Aizawl, was very significant and relevant because the problems currently faced by the State of Mizoram were highlighted and discussed by distinguished scholars. Bounded by two international borders Mizoram, a tiny State in the North-East India, has 404 and 318 kms long borders with Myanmar in the east and Bangladesh in the west respectively. Because of these two international borders Mizoram has an enormous problem with immigrants.

The papers presented and discussed were informative and thought provoking, and these papers may serve as important documents for future reference on Mizoram. Though the efforts were intended to bring out the whole picture on Mizoram concerning the position of illegal immigrants, the attempts, with these papers as a case study, were not exhaustive, yet, certain conclusions may be drawn from these papers:

First, illegal immigrants have entered Mizoram for two major factors: (i) political and (ii) economic.

Accordingly, the immigrants may be termed as political refugees and economic migrants.

Secondly, some Gurkhas who are now treated as permanent inhabitants are descendants of those whom the British government allowed to settle in Mizoram after their retirement from the services.

Thirdly, the Myanmarese came to Mizoram as a result of political persecution and economic reasons.

Fourthly, the Chakmas entered Mizoram, apart from other reasons, following the invitation of some Mizo chiefs for want of subjects.

Fifthly, Riang, known as Bru today, entered Mizoram following the Riang uprising against the Tripura Maharaja in 1940s.

While writing a short introduction, it is appropriate to write in brief about the impact of Gorkha settlement on Mizoram. This is necessary because of the fact that none of the papers dealt with this aspect.

As noted above, the Gorkhas are descendants of discharged military policemen of long service who were originally recruited in Lushai Hills. In course of time, their numbers have increased alarmingly. Therefore, now they are the people to be reckoned with. Scattered at different places all over Mizoram, the Gorkhas have been maintaining identity as a separate community. Therefore, it is very difficult to identify who is the permanent resident or who an illegal immigrant. This kind of social mobilisation amongst the Gorkhas has created a lot of problem for the people of Mizoram. The Gorkha residents, who are considered as permanent inhabitants of Mizoram, have a right to vote and exercise their franchise in elections. Though they do not contest elections with a separate candidate, the Gorkhas always play a significant role in the elections. Recognising the role of the Gorkhas in the society, Kapur Chand, a Nepali merchant at Aizawl was nominated as Member of Legislative Assembly (MLA) in the first ministry ever formed by Ch. Chhunga following his party's (Mizo Union Party) landslide victory in the elections held in 1972. The election was necessitated by the upgradation of Mizo District into Union Territory of Mizoram in the same year. Normally, this community used to cast its votes for a particular candidate enmasse, thus allowing one candidate to win. In this way, the Gorkha community has been playing a decisive and meaningful part in the society. For this reason, some local candidates sometimes put baits to the people with a view to winning their votes. It is needless to say that when Mizo National Front (MNF) started the movement for independence from India in 1966, a number of Gorkhas joined MNF again. On the economic front their contribution is said to be marginal. A few of them run shops in Aizawl and some other places in Mizoram but these do not matter much. What matters rather is the role of the cowherds who supply milk to the city and some other towns. Most of the Gorkhas who live in the outskirts of Aizawl with cows for their milk are generally illegal immigrants who came all the way from Nepal. These groups of people do not constitute any threat to the people of Mizoram economically. However, the threat has come through the multiplication of the Gorkha population in Mizoram. Lastly, the Gorkhas are generally backward due to lack of proper education. There is only one Gorkhali school in Aizawl where they can go up to class X. In spite of this, a number of Gorkhas hold important posts in the government services. After all, the Gorkhas are good friends of the local people and both communities have been living side by side in cordial relationships for a number of years.

Thanks are due to the MAKAIAS for sponsoring seminar and the scholar-contributors for without them the seminar would not have been a success. It may be suggested that this kind of seminar may also be held in other parts of the States in the North-East India, so, as to bring out the real picture of the nature and status of the cross-border movements of people the suggested solutions.

2

The Coming and Settlement of Chakmas

F. Lianchhinga

The Chakmas, who have been passing through very critical phase of their political history, and who have played an important role within India, Myanmar and in their homeland, Bangladesh, require careful consideration. The name 'Chakma' appears to be a variation, as they themselves pronounce the word as Shangma or Shagma. But at present they are officially known as Chakma. Taranatha includes them among the Kuki group[1]. Some think that the name means 'self lover'[2]. Lucien Bernot is of the opinion that it means 'mixed origin'[3]. Hutchinson thinks that they are undoubtedly of Arakanese origin[4], and Risley assigns them to Mongoloid derivation[5]. They are the original inhabitants of the Chittagong Hill Tracts (CHT) of Bangladesh[6]. The Dengawadi Aredfung history of the Arakan kings mentioned the Chakmas for the first time in about A.D. 1118[7]. The real history of the Chakmas began with their first chief Bijoygiri who made terms with the Arakanese kings and settled down in their neighbourhood to the south of the Chittagong District[8]. It was for this reason that the Chakma chiefs remained under the subjugation of the Arakanese kings. Afterwards, the Afghan rulers ruled them for a considerable period of time up to 1666[9]. Then the Moghuls occupied Chittagong Hills in 1761. In that year Chittagong was given to Robert Clive as Zamindary[10]. When the British occupied Chittagong, the Chakmas entered a new stage of history. Henry Varelest, the chief of the Chittagong Council, by a proclamation dated 6th Sraban 1170 M.S. declared the local jurisdiction of the Chakma chiefs to be "All the hills from the Pheni river to the Sangu, and from Nizampur road to the Kuki Raja"[11]. During this period chief Rothangpuia, controlled up to Bawrkawlh tlang; and Mahmuam, Lunginkhar, Saichal and Lawngkawr were under the Mizo chief but the British included them within the East Bengal Province. The Chakmas now inhabit Bangladesh, Myanmar and India. In Myanmar and Bangladesh they are domiciled citizens, whereas in India almost thirty per cent of them constitute refugees and illegal immigrants.

The Chakmas who first footed the Mizoram soil were the captives; only few of them returned after the British occupation, but most of them lived with the Mizo who proselytised themselves to their captors. The second group were the coolies of the Lushai expeditionary forces supplied by Chakma

Kalindi Rani. They landed on Labung on November 17, 1871[12]. But those coolies returned without lingering behind.

Causes of Chakma Immigration into Mizoram

The first Chakma immigration took place around 1895-1905 when chief Zekhupa, son of Vannawla, chief of Lunginkhar (now Bangladesh) occupied Muallianpui Tlang with his subjects along with a few Chakma families[13]. Zakhupa was a Tlanglau chief. By this time another Chakma group also immigrated and settled down on the bank of Kawrpui river. Joying, a leader and his followers, who had the knowledge that there was vacant fertile land within chief Rothanpuia's, began to settle down in the area which was not far from Khanglui (Khojoisuri in Chakma). With this background in view we may now investigate the causes of the coming of the Chakmas into Mizoram.

Economic Cause

The Chakmas, who are in the habit of shifting cultivation, know that there were fertile and cultivable areas within the lands of the Mizo chiefs bordering their settlements and these attracted them. When they came to know that the Mizos prohibited their headhunting practices, they sought for new fertile lands for settlement. So they entered Mizoram with the permission of the Mizo chiefs of Puankhai, Tiante, Pukzing, Phuldungsei, Serhmun, Pharva, Charluitlang and Muallianpui. It is alleged that some of them came to Mizo Hills in order to escape the consequences of the infringement of law[2] and order which they committed under their own chief in East Bengal. Interestingly, the illegal entry of Chakmas was encouraged by the Mizo chiefs themselves. For want of subjects and local taxes they admitted them without prior permission of the government. By and by, the government learnt that there were a large number of illegal immigrants sheltered by the Mizo chiefs so as to get more tax. As a result, in 1928 the government issued a Standing Order that Non-Lushais (Non-Mizos) should pay a Foreigner Tax of Rs. 5 per year to the government[14]. In pursuance of Inner Line Regulation Act, the government again superceded the Notification No. 9104 of August 28,1930 regarding the control of Non-Lushais into Mizoram[15]. This notification mentions that only the indigenous inhabitants and foreigners who had been permitted to reside in the Lushai Hills were allowed to dwell in Mizoram. It further mentions : "The Chakmas and Tripuras have not proved useful settlers. Their presence is inclined to produce litigation.... The settlement of Chakmas, Tripuras and Nepalese is prohibited except with the permission of the Superintendent...". The Standing Order No. 16 of 1928[16] also clearly specified the condition of the

Foreigners thus : "In future all foreigners including Coalas settled in the District will pay taxes as below: " House Tax of Rs. 5 to the government. Two baskets of paddy or Rs. 2 per annum per house to the chief, if they have jhums Rs. 3 per annum to the chief by those who keep cattles for trade in addition to usual Grazing fee to be paid to government". It may be noted further that the British government on temporary basis gave land to a Tangchangya sub-tribe of the Chakmas named Debicharan by cutting off a portion of Bawtlira's land[17]. Again in 1937, the government notified that Non-Lushais should pay a house tax of Rs. 5 per annum to the government[18]. Therefore, owing to lack of foresightedness of the Mizo chiefs, within five decades the Chakmas outnumbered the indigenous people within the Chiefs domains of Vaseitlang, Muallianpui, Tiante, Saizawh, Serhmun, Saisih and Sirte[19]. In 1932, 1933[20] and 1937[21] the government issued orders regarding the Chakma settlements. Occasions, however, might conceivably arise when on a temporary 3 years basis on Forest village or similar settlement basis temporary settlement might be permitted in the low riverine areas near main large rivers in return for Forest road making or inter-village path construction.

Political Cause

A great wave of Chakma infiltration took place from 1936 to 1944. The main reasons were the Second World War and the greediness of the Mizo chiefs. On hearing the mass immigration of the Chakmas the government notified the following principles[22] to be observed in dealing with the Chakmas:

1. Owning to the large number of Chakmas now settled in the South Lushai Hills, most of whom have considerable families, no further applications for settlement will be considered but for the most exceptional reasons.
2. Passes for new separate houses will be considered except where the applicant is (a) the grown-up married son of a Chakma who has been settled for at least ten years in the Lushai Hills; (b) the grown-up married grandson of such settler. In both these cases the applicant himself must also be a permanent resident of the Lushai Hills. Passes for daughters will not be considered. If those marry outside Chakmas, they must go to their husbands villages. If they marry Lushai Chakmas the husband will be covered by the rules above.
3. The site of each Chakma basti will be decided by the Chief in consultation with the Karbari and will be reported to the Circle Interpreter. This site

will not be changed without permission from the Sub-Divisional Officer, and the location of the basti reported for record in his office.

4. The basti shall consist of not less then 15 houses which are to be concentrated on a village site, or along a lane which shall not be more than jhum houses, granaries etc.

5. The Chakmas will make and maintain throughout the year a footpath from their basti to the Chief's village.

6. The rules about cutting jhums on the river banks will be strictly observed and orders from this office will be obtained before any departure is made from these rules.

7. Chiefs will be responsible for the general control of Chakmas in their ram. They will normally work through the Karbari, who will be removable on the recommendation of the Chief if he is found to be either ineffective or of bad character.

8. Mass movement of a whole or the large part of a basti from one Chiefs ram to another will require the sanction of the Sub-Divisional officer or Superintendent. Individual permission of houses and families will be allowed as in Luchai villages. It is certain that some Chakmas entered Mizoram due to the infringement of law and order within the Chakma chief area in CHT. At the same time the Mizo chiefs, as mentioned earlier, were also

solely responsible for admitting the Chakmas in their respective jurisdictions.

Equally, the colonial power was also politically responsible for the coming of the Chakmas into Mizoram. They snatched away some parts of their lands or they abolished some chiefs in order to accommodate some Chakmas. Such cases had occurred in 1934 when the British portioned out Serhmun which was then given to Debicharan, a Tangchangya Chakma. They also transferred Lunginkhar, Saichal, Mahmuam and Bawrkawlh to Chakma chief Ang Mong[23].

Even after independence, the illegal entry of Chakmas continued. This time the political parties were responsible. Like the chiefs who allowed the Chakmas to illegally settle in their domains for the sake of their own good, the political parties allowed them for their party interests. In the first election of Advisory Council in 1948, the Mizo Union party, the only dominant party in Mizoram allowed Chakmas to vote[24]. Again, when the Mizo Autonomous District Council was created, the Mizo Union Party then gave Medhia Chakma a nominated seat. Likewise, the Lushai Hills District (Revenue Assessment) Regulation 1953 exempted the Chakmas form paying the foreigners tax of Rs. 5. Instead, they were allowed to pay Rs. 2 like the Mizo. Meanwhile, the Government of India included the Chakmas of Mizoram in the Scheduled Tribes list in 1956[25]. When the first general election of Lushai Hills Autonomous District Council was held the Mizo Union Party won a landslide victory. This led to the reservation of one nominated seat to the Chakmas. This clearly removed the anxiety of the Chakmas who till then regarded themselves as taxed subjects or aliens. In spite of the fact that the government issued a Standing Order in 1954[26] to check mass infiltration of Chakmas and Tripuras, the public leaders took steps contrary to this. So, none but the Mizo themselves could be blamed for the admittance of the immigrants as citizens of Mizoram.

It may also be noted that installation of the Hydro-Electric Project of Kamafuli river in East Pakistan, now Bangladesh, was also responsible. The dam enundated a large tract of Chakmas inhabited areas. As a result, the poor and ignorant Chakma refugees entered into the neighbouring countries, India and Burma, in 1964. The last mass immigration of foreigners took place during 1980-1984. This was caused by the insurgency in the CHT led by the Hill People Movement of Bangladesh. The writer himself witnessed the events.

Chakma Population

Before 1901, no record has been found regarding the presence of the Chakmas in Mizoram. But, in 1901 census, a few people numbering 128 were mentioned.

It appears that they were the followers of Chief Zakhupa of Muallianpui. Following are the census-wise growth rates of the Chakma population during 1901-1971[27].

Yearly Total Population and Growth Rate of Population Chakma

	Growth	*Rate of Mizoram Percentage*	*In Mizoram.*	*Percentage*
1901	82,434	–	128	–
1911	91,204	10.64	306	139
1921	98,406	7.90	608	98.69
1931	1,24,404	26.42	936	53.94
1941	1,52,796	22.81	5088	443.58
1951	1,96,202	28.42	11435	124.75
1961	2,66,063	35.61	19377	69.45
1971	3,32,390	24.92	22393	15.56

The rapid increase of Chakma population was seriously observed by the sons of soil. The 1981 census operation did not mention the exact number of Chakmas in Mizoram. According to the Government of Mizoram records the number of population within Chawngte Sub-Division (CADC area) show unbiological increase as under[28]:

Group Center	*Population of 1982*	*Population of 1983 (February)*	*No. of Increase 1982-1983*
Chawngte (K.Nagar)	8648	10041	1393
Vaseitlang	4330	6398	2068
Boroponsuri	1896	2559	663
Jarulsuri	1407	1657	250
Damdep	1912	3042	1130
Pharva	2061	2699	638
Total	*20254*	*26396*	*6142*

The percentage of increase during six months - 23.23%.

The Chakmas claim that the actual number of population was 52,000 in 1971 and 71,000 in 1991. If this estimation is correct, it is evident that the number of contracts of Chakmas in Mizoram was quite large.

The periodic census vividly reveals a rapid increase of Chakma immigrants in Mizoram.

Year	*Immigrants*	*Year*	*Immigrants*
1901	198	1961	1937
1911	306	1971	23236
1931	836	1981	39636
1941	5088	1991	51749 Tuichawng & Belpui 52836.
1951	11435		

If the Chakmas' claim is correct, there will be illegal Chakma settlers in Mizoram numbering about 71,000 - 52,836 = 18164.

Conclusion

The historical and political facts regarding the Chakmas in Mizoram are clearly known. The fact is that they were mistakenly admitted as citizens and settled with an institution of local self-government (Autonomous District Council) by the power of the Administration. The land was formerly and originally the land of Mizo chiefs. As a matter of fact, at the time when chicftainship was abolished in Mizoram in 1954, there was one Chakma chief named Lombomui of Lukisuri. He said that the Chakmas settled in Mizoram due to negligence and inadequacy of civil administration. Yet many Chakmas who served as labour force during the Second World War from East Pakistan (now Bangladesh) lingered behind. With the passage of time, the Chakmas also gradually asserted their political rights by making demands for a better status. Before the Chakmas were given a separate Pawi-Lakher Regional Council (P.L.R.C.) Autonomous District councils, the Chakmas belonged to the P.L.R.C. Later, the P.L.R.C. was made into three Autonomous District Councils, viz., Lai, Mara and Chakma Autonomous District Councils. Now the Chakmas, who were illegal immigrants before, have a separate local self-government within Mizoram. Apart from the factors, already mentioned above, responsible for the settlement of Chakmas in Mizoram, mention may also be made of others who were responsible for the creation of the Chakma Autonomous District Council. The Mizo National Front (MNF) movement was responsible. Due to MNF insurgency an anti-Mizo sentiment developed among the Chakmas; and the anti-Mizo movement received approbation of the Center more than the version of the Mizo leaders. For the sake of security, the formation of a separate administrative units in the areas along the East Pakistan border was vital to check the cross-border movement of the MNF underground insurgents. In this respect, the then Administrator of Mizoram and Deputy Commissioner, C.J. Das and A.C. Ray respectively had negative attitudes towards the Mizos and they played vital roles in making the P.L.R.C. into three Autonomous District Councils. The United Legislature Party of Mizoram formed by the Mizo Union and Mizo District Congress Committee did not raise any dissenting voice to the Centre regarding the formation of the Chakma Autonomous District Council. So, whether we like it or not, the Chakmas have now become a separate community with a separate administrative unit within Mizoram.

References

1. Taranatha, *History of Buddhism,* Motilal Banarsidas Publisher, Delhi, 1970, pp. 330-331.
2. Thun Shew Khine, *Rakhine Kiauphiah Detaniah Thet Tangia Tama,* Rangoon 1988.
3. Abdus Sattar, *In The sylvan Shadaws,* Dhaka Academy of Letters, Dhaka, 1983, p. 357.
4. R.H.S. Hutchinson, *The Chittagong Hill Tracts,* Vivek Publishing Co. Delhi, p. 21.
5. H.H. Risley, *Tribes and Caste of Bengal,* Culcutta, p. 154.
6. S.P. Talukdar, *The Chakmas: Life And Struggle,* Gian Publishing House, Delhi, 1988.
7. Abdus Sattar; op.cit., p. 276.
8. R.H.S. Hutchinson, op.cit., p. 22.
9. D.G.E.Hall, *History of South East Asia.* Macmillan Co. London, 1955, p. 424.
10. Ibid.
11. R.H.S. Hutchinson, op.cit., p. 24.
12. T.H.Lewin, *A Fly On The Wheel or How I Help To Govern India,* Tribal Research Institute, Aizawl (Reprint) 1977, p. 265.
13. The information was collected from V. Rothanga, grandson of Zakhup, Saizawh.

14. A.G.McCall, *The Lushai Hills District Cover (1938-1939)*, (Reproduced by H.Raltawna, Deputy Commisioner, Aizawl District 1987-88), p. 492.

15. Ibid, p.76.

16. Col-No.I File No. 8 of 1928 (16.8.1928)

17. Lambamoni, Ex-Chief of Chakma. Interviewed on 10.7.1989.

18. A.G. McCall, op.cit., p. 111.

19. Ibid. p. 492.

20. Ibid. pp. 112,75.

21. Ibid. p. 258.

22. Ibid. p. 492.

23. R.H.S. Hutchinson, op.sit., p. 24.

24. *Chakma Chanchin* by Tribal Research Institute, Aizawl, 1996, p. 51.

25. Ibid.

26. Memo No.G.P. 21/54/52 of 2 July 1954. File No. 12. P of 1932.

27. J.V. Hluna; *A Search for Mizo Identity*, Synod Press, Aizawl, 1983, pp. 244-45.

28. Ibid. p. 246.

3

Riang in Mizoram:
Settlement and its Impact

Lianhmingthanga
J.V. Hluna

Riang is a tribal group who have been settling in Tripura, Mizoram, Manipur, Cachar district of Assam and Chittagong Hill Tracts of Bangladesh. The largest concentration of these people is found in the state of Tripura. In Mizoram, the tribe forms a small minority community which settled only in the western belt of the State bordering Tripura, Cachar District of Assam and Chittagong Hill Tracts of Bangladesh. A census report of 1971 says that there were 9828 souls who spoke the language of Riang. This may roughly be considered as the total number of Riang people at that time. After twenty years or so the number would have increased and now the Riang issue has assumed significant importance in Mizoram.

Nomenclature

The word 'Riang' is a word or term used for the name of the tribe in old records and books. The Riang themselves do not know the meaning of this term nor do they call themselves by this word. It is believed to be the name used by their neighbouring Bengali people for calling them. In his book, 'The Riangs of Tripura', Jagadish Gan. Chaudhury said that the word 'Riang' is derived from the name of a bird Garur which is by Riang dialect Beangma which was corrupted into 'Biang' and then 'Riang'. According to him also, the Uchai tribe of Tripura has another story to tell: that during their migration from Burma-Arakan to Chittagong Hill Tracts, the Riangs moved first and the Uchai followed them. The advance party was called 'Riangsa' and the rear party 'Ulsa' which is now corrupted into Uchai[2]. As long as no other research finding is there, this is quite acceptable. The Government of Tripura also in its community register entered 'Riang' at the end of the name of these tribe members. In the Mizoram Census Report of 1971, 'Riang' is also used for calling this tribe[3]. The Riang call themselves 'Bru' which means man. The term 'Bru' seems to be originated from the term 'Bruha' who was, according to their folktale, their ancestor and leader and who, during their westward movement, led them to their present place of settlement[4]. The Mizos call them by 'Tuikuk' which means 'bathing'. The origin of this term is generally said to be like this—A Mizo traveller while travelling happened to meet a Riang man who was taking bath in a stream and asked the latter to which tribe or community he belonged. The Riang man said in reply, "Tuikungrm" which means 'I am bathing'. Then the traveller heard him saying 'Tukung' and this was corrupted into 'Tuikuk'[5]. The Riang themselves dislike this term and when used they feel annoyed and think of being looked down upon by the Mizo. In return, the Riang call the Mizo by 'Skam' which means 'savage' or 'head hunter'. Now, the use of 'Bru' for calling the Riang has become common among the Mizos. This is due to the work of Christian Missionaries who studied hard the attitude and sentiments of the Riang people. In all the Christian Missionary works, the Riang are recorded as Bru. The use of 'Bru' was also popularised by the Riang themselves when a political movement demanding Autonomous District Council for Riang in Mizoram was started in 1997 in the name of Bru National Army (BNA) or Bru National Liberation Front (BNLF).

The People

From all appearances there is no doubt that the Riang belong to the Mongoloid race, their physical features being scanty hair on face and body, flat nose and face with prominent cheek bone. All anthropological studies on these people point to the Mongoloid character or tradition. They speak a dialect of their own which is very close to the other dialects like: Jomatia, Nowatia Tipra, Uchai of Tripura which fall under one term 'Kokborok'. The dialect of the Riang is also said to be very akin and close to the language of Kacharis and Bodo of Assam. According to Chaudhary, the Riang dialect belongs to the Bodo group of Tibeto-Burman family[6], but Grierson put the Riang language among the fourth group of Mon-Khmer family in which the language of the Khasis is one of them. However, there are some who say that the Riang belong to Kher group of Mongoloid race as certain group of people who are very much like them are still living in Myanmar[7].

Another opinion offered by R.H. Sneyed Hutchinson is that the Riang are the sub-caste of Tippera(Tipras) which according to him are of Kuki origin. Of course, there are certain links or similarities between the Riang and the Kuki (now Mizo) not only in physical features but also in languages[8]. Whatever be the opinion put forwarded by the scholars and writers mentioned, it is the finding made by Chaudhury that is quite reliable and acceptable. According to him, the Riangs belong to Bodo branch of Tibeto-Burman language family. From the branch 'Bodo' there are the Kacharis, Garos, Rabhas, Laungs, Kochs, Dimasas, Chutiyas, Tipras, Riang, Jamatias

Nowatias Uchais, etc[9]. The dialects of these tribes are closely related to one another.

In all the Riang are of two types—one is called Dikhin Riang and the other is Khondol, the former being southern Riang and the latter western Riang. There is no marked difference between the two except minor differences in dialect and female dresses.

The Coming and Settlement

According to the observation of G.A. Grierson, the original homeland of Tibeto-Burman language speakers is somewhere in the North-West China and therefrom they moved towards the Irrawady and the Chindwin and the last wave moved to the South-West and first occupied Garo Hills and then the state of Tripura[10]. Instead, there is also another view that the Riangs moved towards Myanmar, Arakan, Chittagong Hill Tracts and then Tripura. This is evidenced by the presence of Riang tribe in these places. From Tripura, some Riangs moved towards the east crossing Jampui Hill areas and some of them reached the western areas of Mizoram and settled there, while others moved to the Cachar District of Assam. This Riang movement was due to their uprising against the Tripura Maharaja that took place during the 1940s. Some of them are also known to have entered Mizoram from Chittagong Hill Tracts of

Bangladesh where a good number of them are still settling.

The reason for this movement might be due to inter-tribal feuds with the Chakma or most probably due to attraction of a vast unpopulated forest land in Mizoram. Another reason of the Dikkhin Riang migration from Chittagong is also believed to be the construction of Hydro-Electricity Dam at the Karnifuli river which has brought a vast area of land under water. Because of this, many Chakma were also known to cross the border and moved to Arunachal Pradesh. In the case of the Riang, who were at that time small in number, they could somehow manage settlement along the sparely populated areas along the western border of Mizoram with Bangladesh and Tripura. This movement and settlement of the Riang in Mizoram started a few years before 1950 and continued in small hordes or numbers thereafter. The Dikkhin Riang are therefore said to have been settling in the areas of Tlabung and Persang Hill areas of Lunglei District and Darlak village of Mamit District.

The other group of Riang—Khondol (Western), lived mostly in south District of Tripura. When the 20th century began, there came big things that changed the life of many people in the world. It was no exception for the Riang also, among whom emerged a leader. In the year 1942 when the Second World War was being fought, a major incident happened in the community life of Khondai Riang. There was a movement in the name of a religion led by Ratnamani (1892-1943), an immigrant from the Chittagong Hill Tract. When his popularity grew and gained momentum, the Riang leader, Rai got annoyed and feeling jealous, he reported upon Ratnamani's rebellious act—not willing to pay tax to the Maharaja. Since then, Ratnamani and his active followers had to hide in the jungle with whatever arms they possessed. At long last, Ratnamani, thinking that he would soon be arrested, sent word to his followers that they should move eastward where the inhabitants would tell them new religion which they must follow and accept. Soon after 'that, Ratnamani was captured and was known to have been punished with death at the Maharaja Palace. Nine followers of Ratnamani were also to be arrested each of them carrying Rs. 900 on his head.

Following the words of Ratnamani, the nine followers of his went to Jampui Hills and sought the help of K.T. Chawma Sailo[1], a chief of Sabual village. Understanding their miserable condition, K.T. Chawma Salio committed to render all possible help. Then hordes of Khondol Riang left their erstwhile settlement in south Tripura for Jampui Hills and its adjoining areas which fall within north Tripura and some of them reached the Langkaih and the Teirei river valleys of Cachar and of Mizoram. Majority of them settled in the river valley of Deoa. Untill 1920 no Riang settlement was found to the east of Longlorai Hill which is the third Hill Range from Jampui Hills. However, after 20 years or so, in 1939, only a small hamlet of Riang was found in the river valley of Deoa where now a majority of the Riang of north Tripura are settled[11]. So it is certain that the Riang (Khondol) group moved up leaving their homeland in south Tripura due to their strained relation with the Maharaja. Some of them settled in the river valley of Deoa during 1940 to 1960. As the Jampui Hills had already been populated by the Mizo some of them moved further eastward into the river valley of Teirei. Some Riang even crossed over the borders of Tripura and settled in Cachar District of Assam. However, a large section of the Riang people, particularly Khondol Riang, are still settled in the south Tripura Districts mostly in the rural areas. As far as their distribution in Mizoram is concerned, the Riang as a whole live in 35 villages or hamlets in Mizoram. As per the latest record of the Synod Presbyterian Church Office, Aizawl, there are 12 villages in the north Mizoram which are inhabited purely by the Riang. Beside these, some Riang are also known to have settled in some Mizo villages.

The following are the available records of the names of village and their populations[12].

Table: Riang Settlement in Mizo Villages

Sl. No.	*Name of Village*	*No. of Household*	*North/ South*	*No. of Population*
(1)	*(2)*	*(3)*	*(4)*	*(5)*
1.	Darlak	30	North	N.A.
2.	Nalzawl	44	North	200
3.	Bawngva	64	North	291
4.	Mualthuam	20	North	N.A.
5.	Tuirum	56	North	268
6.	Khawhnai	25	North	120
7.	Serhmun	8	North	44
8.	Bunghmun West	12	North	93
9.	Sihthiang	38	North	200
10.	Teirei West	29	North	130
11.	Pangbalkawn	39	North	208
12.	Chhimluang	48	North	88
13.	Chuhvel	10	North	N.A.
14.	Kananthar	15	North	66
15.	Saikhawthlir	7	North	N.A.
16.	Thaidawr	74	North	430
17.	Rotlang West	80	South	380
18.	Phairuangkai	50	South	250
19.	Bolia	78	South	450

Contd.

(1)	(2)	(3)	(4)	(5)
20.	Belthei	64	South	464
21.	Chhumkhum	20	South	90
22.	Zawlpui	55	South	225
23.	Parva II	49	South	297
24.	Saizawh East	30	South	190
25.	Buknuam	32	South	206
26.	Zehtet	82	South	33396
27.	Putlunga Sih	165	South	1123
28.	Kawrthindeng	71	South	390
29.	Saibawh	40	South	290
30.	Zomuantlang	44	North	258
31.	Damparengpui	124	North	1328
32.	Tuipuibari	129	North	140
33.	Tumpanglui	20	North	N.A.
34.	S.Sarali	15	North	N.A.
35.	Tuipuibari Centre	143	North	455
	Total	*1807*		*42065*

Impact of the Settlement

Having highlighted the background history of the tribe, now an attempt will be made to deal with the possible impact of the Riang settlement in Mizoram. Unlike the Chakma tribe, the Riang settlers in Mizoram have never been so aggressive, nor were the known to be very conscious of political or communal feeling in the past against the indigenous Mizo inhabitants. As such there has not been any ill-feeling or problem from them as a community and there was no restriction on their entry into Mizoram by the generic name the 'Riang'. But as the time passed decade by decade, the increase of their population by biological and cross border movement processes, problems have come to surface for the people of Mizoram and now the Riang issue is one of the headaches of the State government. With a sizeable number of population, the Riang settlement here inevitably has some impact on the Mizo people, not only in politics but also in other spheres, which however may be direct or indirect and positive or negative. Let us therefore summarise on the following points:

1. *Socio-Economic*—With an on going civilisation, the Riang also can no longer live a life at par or within the ambit of their tradition. Their socio-culture life has undergone a great change. As they form a small minority community in Mizoram, settled in scattered areas, there cannot be a strong force or influence of any kind for the majority tribe or mainstream. Many of them live and settle in the Mizo villages, where they have to cope with the living style of the Mizo society and follow certain obligations to a great extent. Now, most of the Riang habitations in the interior places are no longer that much remote. They have

been in close contact and mixed up with their neighbouring Mizo people in their day-to-day life. As they belong to a smaller community there cannot be a strong influence of their socio-cultural way of life on the Mizo. Instead, there has been found the trend of transformation of their socio-cultural and traditional way of life, because it is quite natural and as a rule a bigger cultural group is always suppressive or, in other words, it has stronger influence over the smaller cultural group. So there seem not much changes or effects on the Mizo people as far as their socio-cultural traditional set up is concerned. But the members of the two tribes living in close contact or rather mixing with one another has evidently created certain effects on either side. Now, there are many cases of inter-tribal marriages between the two tribes. Here, one of the impacts of the Riang settlement in Mizoram is that it has broadened the marriage market for Mizo boys and girls. In many cases of inter-tribal marriages, the offsprings of the couple also follow suit. Thus, the effect of inter-tribal marriage causes diminishing process in terms of numerical strength of population on the Riang side while the process of population increase is there on the Mizo side.

As far as the Riang's economy is concerned, agriculture by jhum cultivation is their purely basic source of income and daily bread. Now even in the interior places of the Riang habitation in Mizoram, fertile land for jhum cultivation is scarce and their jhum produce has become very poor and self-sufficiency in food production is no longer possible. As the jhum cultivation requires a vast area of land for rotation, the less the cycle, the less fertility of the land with poor productivity. The Riang in Mizoram with such a size of population is certain to have needed and used up a vast area of land. Many of them are even found settling within and around the Tiger Wild Life Sanctuary at Dampa. It is sure that some parts of the forest have been deforested for jhum cultivation. Without cutting the forest it would not have been possible to practise jhumming which is their only means of livelihood. So the direct impact of the Riang settlement here is the shortage of land for jhum cultivation and deforestation of the Tiger Wild Life Sanctuary at Dampa which has been looked after by the State Forest Department.

On the other hand, Jhumming is the only traditional profession of the Riang people; they are very adept and good in this work. The Mizo counterpart will be no match to them. Particularly in sowing, weeding and harvesting works, the Riang lads are swift and skilful. Most of the Mizo in the western belt of Mizoram copied the Riang's traditional method of harvesting paddy, that is, cutting the rice plants, the bundle of which is then threshed in a big basket called Kalong, and thereafter bringing the paddy to the jhum house. In the matter of jhum work, the Riang in Mizoram have formed a good work force. As they live a hard life, they go out in search of work among the Mizo. Many Mizo in the western Mizoram make use of their services not only in jhum cultivation but also in other hard and rough works. Without the presence and the involvement of Riang workers the Mizo in these areas would have faced acute labour problem. Dilligent, perserverent and hard worker, the Riang, therefore, contributed a good labour force which may be said to be a positive impact of their settlement. In the recent past like any other Mizo, the Riang were also, given financial assistance under various schemes by the State Government. Some beneficiaries amongst them in Darlak and Zamuang villages are reported to be very successful in the trade of orange and other crops plantation. Some or a few at Sihthiang village are said to possess and maintain land for permanent or wet cultivation. It is not known how far the product will give self-sufficiency in food and crops in these areas.

Regarding their involvement in the service of Mizoram State Government the contribution of the Riang is very poor. As they are economically backward, it is practically impossible for them to go in pursuit of higher studies. So only a few or countable number of the Riang are found to serve in the State Government offices; none are in the Gazetted Officer Rank which causes not much problem except for a little decrease of employment opportunity in the offices for the Mizo people. This state of condition reflects lack of education among them, which has lowered the literacy rate or level of the State which, however, now stands second in all India.

2. *Religion*—The Riang being animist with some element of Hinduism in their performance of rites and ceremonies, there has been found no effect on the faith of the Mizo people except that their presence in Mizoram has provided a missionary field for different Church organisations and individuals. After their entry into Mizoram most of the Riang, (about 70%), have converted into Christianity. This has undoubtedly raised the number of Christian population in the State. Now, there are many good Christians who can manage Church Service in their own villages. Some of them have also been engaged as Missionary Workers in the field. The Christian Missionaries have rendered valuable services for alround development of the Riang people particularly in the educational field. Now, like others, many Riang boys and girls go to school run by Church organisations. Following is

an extract from the report of Home Mission School under Presbyterian Church[13].

Table: Population, Student and Missionary

Sl. No.	*Name of Village*	*No. of Students in Primary/ Middle Schools*	*Popula-tion*	*Members of Presbyterian Church*	*Missionary Teachers*
1.	Salem Boarding	93	140	140	10
2.	Thaidawr	59	430	191	3
3.	Zornuantlang	58	258	195	3
4.	Sihthiang	35	200	196	3
5.	Dampa Rengpur	124	1328	680	5
6.	Chhimluang South	39	296	79	3
7.	Zehtet	94	393	323	8
8.	Parva II	45	297	250	4
9.	Saibawh	23	494	163	3
10.	Kawrthindeng	48	390	221	3
11.	Buknuam	43	205	1189	3
12.	Putlungasih	37	1023	266	3
13.	Tuipuibari Center	84	2262	80	10
14.	Tuirum	–	305	260	–
15.	Bunghmun	–	73	73	
	Total	*782*	*8094*	*4306*	*61*

From the available records being kept by the Presbyterian Church, the number of students in the Middle and Primary Schools is only 698, and out of the total population of 8095, the Presbyterian Church has 3306 faithfuls.

It may also be noted that besides the number of villages shown above, there are some more villages from where no report has been received, and for this reason the percentage of Christian members will possibly be higher than 70 per cent. As many are still in the camps in Tripura, the correct figure of Christian population is not possible to obtain.

3. *Politics*—With a fairly large size of population, the Riang have now played an important role in Mizoram politics. Even with their scattered distribution in Mizoram, the votes of the Riang play a pivotal role in winning election in some constituencies like Kawrthah, Zawlnuam and Phuldungsei. As such, the political parties in Mizoram run a race to win over the Riang propel for their votes. Not to speak of Village Council of the Tiang themselves, two nominated seats of Members of Legislative Assembly (MLA) were allotted to the Riang Community. V. Lalnunzira and Zoduha were the nominated MLAs during 1979-1984 and 1987-1987 respectively. Some villages populated purely by the Riang such as

Thaidawr, Tuipuibari, Dampa Rengpui, Zehtet, etc. are said to have their own Village Councils. In the year 1991, among the Riang youth there was a feeling to form a student body or organisation, which would represent and organise movements for their community's interests. As a result, the Union was formed in July 1991 with Sawibunga as its President and Biakmawia of Dampa Rengpui and Bruno as its Vice President and General Secretary respectively. Later in 1993, the name of the Union was changed to Bru Student Association (BSA). The Bru Student Association then started to play an active role for the cause of their community. In 1993 itself, there appeared the demand for a reserved L.A. seat for the Riang people. The Government could not concede the demand. Since then, there grew amongst the Riang a feeling of deserving a political status so that they could safeguard their identity and community's interests. The feeling of the Riang people in Mizoram is said to have been nurtured and aroused by some veteran politicians in Tripura which has a number of M.L.As and even M.P. from the Riang community. A number of meetings and conferences were convened in and even outside Mizoram which some leaders from Tripura are said to have attended. In course of time, the Riang movement gained momentum and in September-October 1997, the threat of living in Mizoram spread among them and as a result a mass of them left their villages or hamlets in Mizoram for Tripura where they have been accomodated in camps as refugees[14]

Some youth went underground in the name of Bru National Liberation Front (BNLF) and took up arms training at Buhban Hill in Bangladesh. In the wake of their mass migration to Tripura, the BNLF has launched Operation and the following are the sequence of incidents[15]

(a) One Forest Guard, Lalzawmliana was killed by BNLF on 21st October, 1997 at Dampa Wild Life Sanctuary.

(b) M.A.P. Personnels were ambushed and shot at on the road between Kawnpui west and Tuipuibari II on 23rd July, 1998. No casualty.

(c) Two staff of P.H.E., Mizoram Government, were kidnapped by BNLF at Ansuri on 15th April, 2002.

(d) One School Teacher, Lalnunfela of Vanghmun village was kidnapped by BNLF on 19th April, 2002, a week after kidnapping the two P.H.E. staff.

(e) 7 MAP personnels were ambushed and killed at Bandiasora under Lunglei District on 30th June, 2000.

Now representatives of the Riang Welfare Association (RWA) and BNLF have had talks with

Government of Mizoram. Initially the demand put up by BNLF was Autonomous District Council or the Riang which had been turned down by the Government. As known, the talk now centres round the genuine number of Riang residents in Mizoram and their rehabilitation after laying down the arms and eschewing violence, so that negotiation can be continued and held in an atmosphere of understanding and goodwill. Thus, the rapid increase of Riang population in Mizoram has been a real concern to the State Government and the people as well. The demand of an Autonomous District Council (ADC) or Regional Council (RC) by the Bur National Liberation Front (BNLF) has been turned down by the State of Mizoram out and out. In spite of this, talks are on between the two groups to find an amicable settlement; but it is unlikely that the Government of Mizoram will concede anything better than the return of the genuine Riang residents of Mizoram who had left it for Tripura in 1997.

Conclusion

From the foregoing pages, we can assume that the Riang have been settling in Mizoram for the past 50 years or so. Due to inaccessibility of their place of habitation at Tripura along the border areas of Tripura, Cachar District of Assam and Bangladesh they are lagging for behind the mainstream of the State since development schemes could not be implemented easily among them. People use to say that the Riang are backward because of their traditional semi-nomadic habit as they moved and migrated from one place to another at a short interval. This can be true in one sense but is not acceptable wholly, because we know that the Riang, like any other people, have the same wants and the same needs. For fear of Maharaja's retribution, they moved out; and in search of peaceful settlement and fertile forest for jhum cultivation they crossed the border here and there and have settled along the river valleys, never on the hill tops which are mostly beyond the reach of development and civilisation. In Mizoram, the Riang lived peacefully with the Mizo without any hint of communal tension or trouble. Unfortunately, however, since the end of the millennium, a new chapter has opened on the relations between the two communities. After fifty years of peaceful settlement in Mizoram, the Riang left their homesteads and crossed the border towards Tripura during September-October 1997. The Government of Tripura arranged make-shift camps and accommodated them in six camps. It is heard from a reliable source that the Riang refugees in the camps live a hard life. Many of them have died of epidemic diseases. They are longing for their homes in Mizoram and as such many of them had a clandestine return. This is evidenced by the latest report of Home Mission Teachers-cum-Evangelists of Prcsbytcrian Church. While there is not much to say of the effect or changes on the socio-cultural pattern of the mainstream, the Riang settlement for the past fifty years has caused destruction of vast areas of forest land that has gone to their share. And now the Riang community, having some ethnic feeling, has started a seperatist movement, demanding political status which the State Government is not likely to accept. So the settlement of the Riang here has caused an undesirable effect creating major political and contentious issues in the State of Mizoram.

References

1. A.K. Saikia, *Mizoram Census Hand Book,* Nelys Printing Pvt. Ltd, Culcutta, 1971., p. 157
2. Jagadish Gan. Chaudhury, *The Riangs of Tripura,* Department of Welfare for Scheduled Tribe and Scheduled Caste, Government of Tripura, 1983., p. 5.
3. The Mizoram Census Report, 1871.
4. Tribal Research Institute, *A Brief Account of Riangs in Mizoram,* United Press, 1986, Aizawl, p. 2.
5. Ibid., p. 8
6. Jagadish Gan. Chaudhury, op.cit., p. 11.
7. G.A.Grierson, *Language of North Eastern India - A survey* Vol-I (Reprint), Goual Offset Printers, Delhi, 1987., p. 1.
8. R.H. Sneyed Hutchinson, *Chittagong Hill Tracts,* (Reprint) Lakhsmi Printing Works, Delhi, 1978., p. 36.
9. Jagadish Gan. Chaudhury; op.cit., p. 10.
10. G.A. Grierson, op.cit., p. 1.
11. Rev. Hnehliana, *Tuikuk, Riang, Bru-Manuscript unpublished,* n.d., p. 4.
12. Synod Presbyterian Church Office Record (Extract copy).
13. Synod Presbyterian Church Office, Record.
14. This is as per information collected from V.Lalnunzira, former MLA.
15. As per report of SP, CID, Office.

4

Settlement of Gorkhas

K.L. Pradhan

The present paper tries to analyse in detail the Gorkha immigration and settlement in the State of Mizoram from the later part of nineteenth century. The Gorkhas who settled down permanently in the State before 1950 and their descendants did not face any troubles from the natives as well as from the Government. Before 1980s there was no restriction at all for them in regard to trade, employment, higher education, post-matric scholarship, land settlement etc. It was in mid-1980s that the permanent Gorkha settlers began to face these problems. The main reason behind this was the recent illegal infiltration of the Gorkhas form Nepal and elsewhere who were (are) engaged as labourers, cowherds, lumberjacks etc. Since there were (are) no specific norms to differentiate between the permanent Gorkhas settlers and the illegal infiltrators, it was obvious to the natives and the government to classify all the Gorkhas as foreigners. Mizoram is situated at the corner of the North-East India. It is flanked on the east and south by Myanmar and Chittagong; on the north by Cachar district of Assam and Manipur and on the west by Tripura and Bangladesh. As per Census of India-Marzoam, 2001, the total population of the state is 8,91,058. The demographic features of the population show that the density of population is 40.8 individuals per sq. kms[2].

The latest literacy survey of India indicated Mizoram as the second highest among the Indian States.*The people of India, Vol. XXXIII* shows that there are 18 communities, fourteen scheduled caste, nine scheduled tribes and two other communities. The Gorkha has been classified in one of the eighteen communities[3].

Movements of Gorkhas

The history of Gorkha movement in the State of Mizoram began towards the beginning of the nineteenth century. They initially came form Nepal and later from Derjeeling, Sikkim and other parts of India. The reasons behind their movements have been varied in nature from time to time. It may be shortage of food, lack of employment, political persecution or urge for military adventures. It is presumed that the main reason for their coming to this part was the allurement of military adventures[4]. The Anglo-Gorkha War (1814-16) left a lasting impression upon the East India Company. Sir Charles Matcalf summed up the contemporary opinion of the Gorkha soldier as 'none ever displayed so much bravery in action, so much system and so well timed and confidence.... We have not met with an enemy who has decidedly shown great bravery and greater steadiness than our troops'[5]. In course of the war, an English officer himself developed for the intrepid Gorkha an admiration, even fondness; that was to outlive British's imperial connection with India. The two Gorkha regiments (Nurserri and Sirmur) that had been raised under the British colours had proved successful[6]. In early 1825, at the height of the Anglo-Burmese War (1824-26) Lt. Gen. Edward Paget, Commander-in-Chief of the British Army, proposed to raise more Gorkha regiments for Bengal Native Army[7]. Fully aware of the existing caste prejudice in Bengal Army, one of the British Officials spoke of the advantage of the Gorkha soldiers that 'they are by far the best soldiers in Asia and if they were made participators of our reknown in arms, I conceive that their gallant spirit emphatic of Madhesis (plain people) and unadulterated military habit might be relied on for fidelity and our good and regular pay and noble pensions establishment would perfectly serve to counterpoise the influence of nationality'[8]. In spite of all these appreciations, the British government could not enrol the Gorkha youth in British army openly due to strong opposition from the Nepalese government. Yet, the British illegally engaged some middlemen to lure the Gorkha youth with various promises and facilities. By 1902, there were ten Gorkha regiments in the British Indian Army.

The official records of the Government clearly show that the Gorkha migrations and settlement in Mizoram began in 1891, after the permanent forts were constructed at Aizawl and Lunglei. However, they had set their feet on the soil much earlier then British mercenaries. The expansion of the territories by the Kuki, Chin-Lushais towards the south and south–cast led to the confrontation with the people of plains[9]. The Lushais had been raiding into the British territories for which the latter had to send several military columns during 1824-44. In spite of these the Lushais continued to raid the plains of Sylhet, Cachar, Manipur and Chittagong. To check the raids on the frontiers, the British government sent Lister's expedition in 1849; Nuthall's expedition in 1869; and two columns of military expeditions in 1971-72. The Chin-lushai expedition (1889-90) was a reprisal measure against the offending Lushais chiefs and also to establish fortified stocade in the Hill[10]. The British India army comprised of 400 Gorkha soldiers of 2/2 Gorkha Regiments and 9 Bengal Infantry under Brig. Tregear reached Lungiei via Demagiri (Tlabung). Similarly, the soldiers belonging to the Surma Valley Military Police (SVMO) and 2 and 3 Gorkha regiments under the commands of Superintendent Dally, Capt. Loch and Lt. G.H. Cole entered Aizawl after subjugating the hill chiefs[11]. By now British government was fully convinced that the only effective method of protecting the frontiers was the establishment of fortified posts and the Hills. Earlier in 1872, Col. Lewin strongly recommended to establish a firm and permanent government machinery in the hills. He even urged the government to set up a series of Gorkha villages along the frontiers between the plains and the hills for proper demarcation of the boundary. He stated that 'the country where these villages were located had previously been uninhabited through fear of marauding Lushia and my idea had been to establish there good stocade villages of courageous stiff necked people of Gorkha who should serve as buffer between the Mong Raja's territories and independent Lushais to the east. The Gorkha colonies were accordingly set up on the bank of river Myani, a north affluent of Karnafuli (now in Bangladesh)[12].

During the course of expedition, Col. Skinner selected Aizawl for the construction of a permanent post in north Lushai Hills in 1889-'90. The fort was garrisioned with 200 armed personnel of the Surma Valley Military Police later named as the 1st (L.H.) Assam Rifles. Thus the foundation for the future district headquarters was laid down. Similarly, Gen. Tregear, with his Frontier Military Police built a permanent post at Lunglei in mid-1889. And in 1889 for better administration and control the north and south Lushai Hill were amalgamated[13].

Beginning of Gorkha Settlement

In 1891-'92 peace was restored in and around the forts. Expansion and developmental works began at Aizawl and Lungiei. For better and smooth functioning of the government machinery and also to meet the basic human needs, the Britishers required man-power like traders, lumberjacks etc. Since the nature of the works were new to the natives, the Gorkhas were accordingly employed for these jobs, and thus began their settlement in Mizoram. The first Gorkha families who settled down permanently in 1889-90 were found in Maubawk, Khagdiya (Rangvamual), Bawngkawn and Kolasib. However, as per government records, their settlement in Mizoram began in 1891[14]. The Chin Hills Regulation Act which came into force in 1896 strictly prohibited the non-Lushais to reside within the district except with the permission of the Superintendent of Lushia Hills[15]. Yet from the beginning of the 20th Century there was a rapid increase in the numbers of non-Lushai settlers in Mizoram. In the case of the Gorkhas, they were the direct descendants of discharged military policemen of long services with good conduct in the battalion originally recruited in Lushai Hills and milk sellers. Initially they settled down at Aizawl, Sairang,

North Vanlaiphai, Lunglei, Demagiri or around 45 miles Dwarband Road (now Thingdawl)[16]. Gradually they shifted to other villages like Buaklunailuak, Bairabi, Chhimluang, North Chaltlang, Kawnpui, Sialsuk, Thenzawl, Tlangnuam, Tuikhawvengthar, Bualpui, Neihbawi, Vairengtc etc. However, the Gorkhas settled in many of these villages cannot be traced. Many of them died heirless and the heirs of others have become Mizo[17].

Within Aizawl town areas, the settlements of the Gorkhas were found in Survey Tilla (now Dinthar-II); Sriman Tilla (now Zotlang); Kemabawk, Bawngkawn, Venghlui, Khatla lane. The Gorkhas once permanently settled felt at home. They found the climate, topography, terrain, flora and fauna akin to that of their original home Nepal.

The natives too resembled them as most of the Gorkhas belong to the Mongoloid stock. The Gorkhas had in no time adjusted themselves with the natives as a result of the bond of friendship and brotherhood that developed[18].

Apparently, the Gorkhas were not allowed to reside or settle down outside the surcharge areas, yet it was the native chiefs who were eager to have them in their villages. They even requested the Superintendent of Lushai Hills to grant special permission to the Gorkhas to settle in their villages.

Accordingly, one or two Gorkha families were given permission to settle in some Lushai villages[19]. The retired Gorkha personnel of the police and Military were allotted considerable portion of lands for dwelling and cultivation purposes. It is interesting to note that some of them were even awarded the privileges and power at par with the native chiefs. For example, Dhojbir Rai was awarded the holdings of the whole areas of Survey Tilla, Sriman Tai to Sriman Tilla; Singbir Rai with holdings to Chawnchhim (Champhai); Laisingh I am to Hriangmual and Joybahadur in Tuienhnar Leilet Settlement[20]. The Gorkhas proved to be worthy residents. They earned good names for themselves and for the states. In various spheres of development they were regarded as the pioneers in the fields of wet rice cultivation, horticulture, animal husbandry; they also contributed in town development, road construction, education etc. It is recorded that in 1898, the Government had started wet rice cultivation at Champhai with the help of Gorkha pensioners and the Santalis. And in 1904 Sukrim Bahadur Thapa (Bura) was engaged as instructor for rice cultivation at Zote village[21]. The terrace system of cultivation in the State was also introduced by the Gorkhas. In course of time, the appointment of a Gorkha Maujadar at Aizawl became effective for the purpose of exercising some administrative coordination over the Gorkha inhabitants within the surcharge area and for the purpose of collecting foreigner's taxes on a commission of the Mauhadar. Those Gorkhas who settled down under a Chief's control were subjected to ordinary Lushai customs and the Chief's order. And whenever cases involving Gorkha customs were tried by the native Chiefs in Aizawl surroundings, the Maujadar was to be present for consultation of the customs[23]. It is recorded that in Aizawl sub-division, 25 of the taxed houses belonged to the Gorkha permanent settlers near Aizawl and cultivators in North Vanlaiphai[24].

Panchayat and Social Organisations

When the institution of Gorkha Maujadar was abolished a Gorkha Panchayat was established at Aizawl. Rules and regulations were laid down with the "intention to give right of control of their social customs with the Gorkha community as far as possible with the least interference by the Magistrate of the District". The Gorkhas having mutual dispute among themselves to be referred to the Gorkha Panchayat at Aizawl. It was represented by Loham Chhetri, Joy Bahadur, Randhoj Rana and others. Similarly, Gorkha Panchayats at 45 miles (Dwarband Road) and other villages were established in due course[25]. At present it has 13 Goan Panchayats all over Mizoram with its headquarters at Aizawl. When the institution of Village Council was introduced in 1954, the Gorkhas were represented fairly through elections or nominations. Some of them were even elevated to the post of Village Council President[26]. Apart form the Panchayat, the Gorkhas had formed various socio-political organisations. Though the exact date of their inception is obscure, but they worked for overall welfare and other related problems for the community. The Nari Samaj (Women's Association) formed way back in the District Council time played a vital role to uplift the women and to eradicate the social evils that existed in the society. The Mizoram Gorkha Youth Association Established in 1976 following the pattern of Young Mizo Association became popular and it plays an important role in bringing the youth together and determines to preserve the social and cultural life of the community. The Gorkha Students' Union which was formed in 1971 also plays a dominant role for the inclusion of the Nepali Language in Eighth Schedule of the Indian Constitution as well as for overall development of education among the Gorkha community[27] · When the question of their identity cropped up in early 1980, the leaders of the community appealed to the government to recognise the permanent Gorkha inhabitants as one of the tribes and extend the facilities at par with the natives[28]. Accordingly, the government ordered a state-wide census for the Gorkhas residing in Mizoram with a view to identifying the permanent inhabitants and illegal Nepali infiltrators to confer certain facilities. On the basis of the census, the government extended some benefits to the permanent Gorkha inhabitants and their descendants who have been in Mizoram from prior to 26 January 1950[29]. "The newly acquired social and legal status" expressed in the editorial of local Newspaper (English) "may very likely boost morale of the Gorkhalis, born and bred in the State and inspire a new sense of belongingness to Mizoram and the society. Moreover, the permanent resident Gorkhalis in Mizoram have deserved the conferment of the status"[30]. But the happiness did not last long. The Students Joint Action Committee vehemently opposed the conferment and pressed the Government to repudiate it. The Government had reluctantly issued another notification rescinding the previous order[31]. Inspite of this, efforts are being made with the Government to reconsider the cause of the permanent Gorkha inhabitants. The present government appears to be much sympathetic towards the plight of the community which hopes to acquire the long cherished aspiration of the Gorkahas in the days to come[32].

References

1. Lalrinmawia, *Mizoram - History And Cultural Identity,* New Delhi, 1995., p. 1.

2. Census of India, Mizoram.

3. Singh, K.S. (Gen. Ed), *People of India - Mizoram Vol XXXIII,* Calcutta 1995, pp. 54-64. The opposition factions were sometime expelled from the State. In 1806 and 1845 the factions who opposed the ruling families were persecuted or compelled to leave Nepal.

4. Hodgson, B.H, *Essays on The Language, Literature And Religion of Nepal And Tibet,* Reprint, New Delhi, 1972. Hodgson records that "the Gorkhas see in foreign service nothing but the prospect of glory...".

5. Thompson E. and Garratt G.T., *Rise and Fulfilment of The British Rule in India,* Oxford 1945, p. 256. In the same documents it is recorded that with a force of less than 16,000 men the Gorkhas fought the British army of 46,200 men whom 4557 were European.

6. Duncun, Forbes, *Johney Gorkhas,* New Delhi 1974, p. 54.

7. Hussain, Imdad, *Problems of Defence, N.E. Frontiers,* Guwahati 1975, pp. 13-45.

8. Pradhan K.L., *Brain Hodgson at the Kathmandu Residency,* 1825-43, New Delhi, 2001, p. 35. Movements of any individual (Nepali) without prior permission of the Govt. was restricted. Violation of it resulted in confiscation of property, imprisonment etc. For details: Stiller L., *"The Silent Cry; The People of Nepal,* Kathmandu 1976, pp. 46-80.

9. *North and North-Eastern Frontiers Tribes of India.* Compiled by the Army Headquarter, New Delhi, 1983, pp. 235-242.

10. Ibid. Also see for details of expeditions in McCall A.G., *Lushai Chrysalis,* Reprint, Culcutta, 1977, pp. 24-66.

11. Reid, A.S., *Chin-Lushia Land,* reprint Culcutta, pp. 13-224. On deployment of the Gorkha soldiers, Reid pointed out that "I allude to the Gorkhas who constitute a most important element in the native army of India, but more on account of their general execellent military qualities and special unrivalled aptitude for hill fighting than on that of their number.... This small force is, I venture to say, allowed to be among the cream of the Bengal infantry.... "*Also see Collection of Correspondences, 1890-1896, Aizawl, 1890,* p. 104.

12. Lewin, Thomas, *A Fly On The Wheel,* Reprint Culcutta, 1977, p. 299. Lewin further stated that "I had formed a high opinion of the little Gorkhas, who under Col. Macpherson, had done the fighting of the expedition, and I obtained permission to send to Nepal and get immigrants form there to colonzie my frontier waste".

13. Nunthara, C.' *Mizoram Society and Policy,* New Delhi, 1996, p. 56.

14. Mizoram State Archives Records, No. 72 (Diary of the Commandant, Frontier Police Battalion Dr., 4th April and 2nd May, 1891). The Diary clearly shows that the Gorkha families were comfortably settled down with extensive garden at Tuihhawng.

15. McCall A.G., *The Luskai Hills District Cover,* Reprint, Calcutta, 1977, p. 104. Also see Chatterji's Mizoram

Under The British Rules p. 313, "These Gorkhas after their retirement from the Army and the Police force, took Lushai Hills as their homelands with their heart and soul and settled there".

16. Ibid.
17. *The Gorkhas of Mizoram, Vol. 1.* Aizawl 2001. p. 100 (Appen. IV).
18. Ibid. p. 15.
19. The Superintendent of Lushai Hills Order No. 31 of 1922 (published by mizo lch Vai Chanchin, 1932, p. 33. It is recorded that "I have been asked several Chiefs to allow settlement of Gorkhalis in their villages". The present orders permit settlements only at or near Aijal, champhai Vanlaiphai.
20. McCall, A.G., op.cit. pp. 103-112. Also see an article of Thangthiauva *"History of Champhai Centenary Souvenir,* 1990.
21. Pachuau Thangvunga, *History Of Wet Rice Cultivation',* published in Champhai Centenary Souvenir, 1990, pp. 78-79.
22. McCall, A.G. op.cit. p. 120. The Government of Assam's order No. 1578 (Revenue Department) dt. 21.5.1932.
23. Ibid. p. 173.
24. Lalrinmawia, op.cit. p. 92.
25. McCall, op.cit. pp. 176-180.
26. The first ever Village Council President was Bir Bahadur Limbu(L) in 1958 and first nominated member was Ranjan Thapa (L) of Venglai Kolasib.

27. For details of activities of the various Socio-Political organisations of the Gorkha in Mizoram, see Kundu, Naveen Kumar, *'Gorkha'* Published in People of India-Mizoram, op.cit. pp. 50-644. Due to their long stay in Mizoram, they supported and helped the cause of the Mizo National Front movement from 1966 in one way or other. Some of them are still alive while others cannot be traced. It was due to this very reason that the QUOT MIZORAM ORDER of 1982 issued by MNF ordering all outsiders to leave Mizoram by 21 June, 1982, was not extended to the Gorkhas who were residing in Mizoram prior to 1966.

28. The Government of Mizoram's Order No. J.11012/2/89 Pol dt. 3 May, 1989. As per Census of 1951, there were 3,468 Gorkha individuals in Mizoram while it is only 4455 as per the Approved Census of Gorkhas in Mizoram vide Memo No. F.22015/85/94-HM-Vol II, 17th May, 2001.

29. The Government of Mizoram Notification issued Vide Memo No. J-20011/102/83-POL (SCT) Dated 3 February, 1992. It reads as "The Government is pleased to extend certain benefits as indicated in Mizoram prior to 26th January , 1950, with immediate effect ;
    (a) Granting of Post-Matric Scholarship.
    (b) Extension of facilities in the matter of education, land settlement certificates including transfer of ownership, employement and trade and commerce on par with their Mizo counterpart.
    (c) Issue Permanent Residential Certificates.

    For the purpose of extending the above facilities the Census of Gorkhas who were permanently residing in Mizoram prior to 20.02.1950 as furnished by the

Deputy Commissioner is to be taken as the basis for the genuineness of their claims."

30. Highlander, (English Daily Newspaper) of 10 February 1992. (See the Editorial).

31. Government of Mizoram Notifications No.op.cit. dt. 15 November, 1992.

32. The Mizo National Front Assembly Election, 1998 Manifestos, in which the party promised for the Gorkha community if they form the Government as:
    (a) As per Indian Constitution and Ministry of Law Notifcation No. SRO. 385 of 10 August, 1950, the permanent Gorkhas settlers shall be given the status of other Backward Classes and extend all the facilities enjoy by this section of people on par with other Indian States.
    (b) The Mandal commission recommendations once accepted by the Government shall be applied to the Gorkha Community.
    (c) The District Council Rules and Regulations adopted by the Government in regard to land, issue of Pass Periodica Patta and Land Settlement Certificate would continue.
    (d) As per Peace Accord of 1986, The Gorkha Community shall be included in Mizoram State Minority List and their rights and privileges will be protected.

5

Myanmarese in Mizoram since the beginning of the Twentieth Century A.D. to the Present

Sangkima

One very serious question at issue now facing the whole world today is the illegal migrations of people from one country to another. This problem has now affected every country in one form or the other. However, in this regard, some countries like Australia, Canada, the European countries, the United States of America, India etc. are perhaps more vulnerable than other countries because they are more sought havens by the asylum seekers.

In matters relating to the cross-border movements of the people, the situation in India's North-East is very much alarming and distressing because all the states in this region are bounded by the international borders. However, the magnitude of the impact of the movements upon the States differs from one State to another.

Mizoram, one of the seven sister-states in the North-East India is much muddled by the same issue because it has an international border of 404 kms with Burma, now known as Myanmar[1]. Myanmar, an independent country in the Eastern portion of mainland South Asia, has an area of 676,577. In 1989 its official name was changed from the Union of Burma to the Union of Myanmar and it is the northernmost of the Southeast Asian countries bordering Mizoram of India in the northeast.

When India and Myanmar became part of the British Empire in 1858 and 1885 respectively there was no international boundary between the two countries as we have today. The people then mod freely from one country to another. But the situation changed when both countries became sovereign states. Henceforth, the two countries have to observe the international norms by preventing or restricting, among other things, the free cross-border movements of the people of the two countries. Consequently, the matters which were earlier a non-issue have now become an international concern.

With this background in view, a brief attempt has been made in this paper to underline the factors which were responsible for the coming of the Myanmarese into Mizoram during the period under review. The study is very relevant and significant as well because the coming of these people has, to a certain extent, affected the lives of the people in Mizoram in various ways.

The People

In this study, the people being investigated are loosely classified into three categories.

The first category are those who speak 'Mizo' as their language and as such they are commonly known as 'Mizo-Group'. During the course of their migration, this group of people arrived in the present Mizoram but in course of time, a number of them went back to Myanmar under various circumstances.

The second category are those people whose dialects are variously different from that of the Mizo dialect which is now a lingua franca in Mizoram. They are otherwise known as 'Chin-Group'. Unlike the Mizo-Group, they are the natural citizens of Myanmar.

The third category are the Myanmarese (Burmese) themselves whom the Mizo call as 'Kawl'[2].

The nature of the coming of these different categories of people, is, however, purposely different from one another.

It may be noted that this paper is perhaps the first of its kind because till now no serious work of this nature has been available. Hence, the paucity of source material is obvious. Therefore, interviews with knowledgeable persons who have come from Myanmar and settled in Mizoram are important sources of information. Literary sources are also used sparingly.

The Coming and Settlement of the People

The Mizo-Group

As noted above, this group of people migrated back to Mizoram under various circumstances. But before we proceed further, it is necessary to know as to why the Mizo group returned to Myanmar from Mizoram and how they were accepted as citizens of Myanmar.

The return of the Mizo to Myanmar began from the beginning of the twentieth century and this lasted till the end of the Second World War. In Myanmar the Mizo are officially known as 'Lushai' and they became citizens in 1950. They returned to Myanmar in three successive waves. The first wave was led by Chief Zahuata of the Hualngo family, who, having reached Mizoram, was badly defeated twice by his adversaris. Having then found his position insecure he went back to Myanmar to rebuild his old and native village Seipui in about 1850.

The second wave took place during the period between the beginning of the twentieth century and the first half of the same century. To begin with, in 1910, a few Zangiat and Zahau families re-entered Myanmar and settled at Myohla village[4]. They were very helpful when the other groups reached there[5]. Ekthawla[6], commonly known in the locality as "Kapmawia pa" and his family, from Hmunhmeltha, arrived in Myanmar followed by Thanghangi and Rinlohva the next year. They took temporary shelters from Hriangtlang village. Some 30 households moved into Myanmar to build a new village at Samuat, but due to strong objection raised by chief Vanhmuanga, the sojourners then diverted their direction and reached Kalemyo area where they founded a new settlement called Lehpangkung[8]. This was the first Mizo village ever established by the Mizo themselves in Myanmar.

In 1910 some 10 families led by Suakdaia left Hmunhmeltha and joined their brethren in Myanmar. This group also built a new village called Natchilung, now known as Tuivar. The next year more than 100 families left Mizoram for Myanmar and scattered at various place. Thus, by 1922, the Mizo built four villages of their own. They were: Lehpangkung, Tuivar, Kapa colony and Thawma village[9]. During

1923-24 four more hamlets were raised. They were: Puikhung and Phulzuan, founded by Pahranga and Sapchhawna respectively. Lalauva and Saltea also set up the villages which were named after them[10].

In 1926 and 1927 Satliana, an ex-service man, and Sapchhawna with Rev. Tuahhranga also established modern Inaigoong and Tahan townships respectively. According to one information Tahan township is now having more than 1000 Mizo households. Generally speaking, the people continued to move, and those who had been there before the war came back to Mizoram to found a temporary settlement. The third wave took pace soon after the War was over. The majority of them moved back during the year 1945-55 and most of them settled down in and around Kalemyo and Tamu areas. Hence, when census was held in 1990, the report was surprising that out of the total population of 252441 in Kalemyo, almost half of the population (45%) belonged to Mizo proper[11]. Thus, the Mizo who are now found in Myanmar are, in fact, the offshoots of the people who had moved into Myanmar at different periods of times. It may be noted further that the people continued to move there to settle down even during the decade of the 1960s.

Meanwhile, the Mizo who were not yet recognised as citizen of Myanmar had to suffer a lot from the government. The problem was so sensitive and serious because it could affect the fate of about 500 Mizo soldiers who had been enlisted before the independence of Myanmar in 1948. In spite of this fact, encouraged by the distinguished and exemplary services performed by the Mizo in the army in 1950, the government recruited more Mizo in the army. But this time, due to the exigency of the case, the government solved the citizenship problem by issuing the Order[12] which has recognised the Mizo born or domiciled in Myanmar as citizens of Myanmar. As a result, the Mizo group have now become real citizens of Myanmar.

However, the citizenship given to the Mizo became doubtful once again when section 2(4) of the Chin Special Division Act 1948 was amended in 1957. According to this amendment, the clause, "Chins of the adjoining areas" was dropped and this automatically withdrew the citizenship of the Mizo. But due to the timely intervention of the Lushai Welfare Organisation which was formed on 18-19 May, 1962, the Revolutionary Council then restored the citizenship to the Mizo. This came in force from 30th November, 1962. Then they were officially recognised as "Burma National Lushais"[13]. But the problem did not end here.

In 1959, for the first time in the history of Myanmar, the Government issued the National Registration Card throughout the country. Every citizen including the Mizo was registered. Following this move, the government then felt the need to know the exact number of the registered Mizo who had made his entry into Myanmar before 23rd March, 1963. In pursuance of this, the government, on 6th April, 1963, ordered what was called the "Ma Ma Operation". Divided into six groups, the operators visited the areas where the Mizo lived, and they pressed upon the Card the seal which says "Myanmar Taingzintal Luseii" which means "Lusei of Myanmar"[14]. With this, the question of "doubtful citizen" came to an end.

The Mizo returned to Myanmar for three definite reasons. First, they found life in Mizoram very difficult and they expected a better and even an easier living condition in the plains of Myanmar. Secondly, they expected to improve their economic conditions by doing wet-rice-cultivation in the plain areas. They were tempted by what had been done at Champhai in Mizoram. Thirdly, the Khampat tradition, as noted above, had a great and sentimental influence upon them. Many really believed the Khampat tradition to come true and that they themselves would be the fulfilment of the legend. It is reported that by the time when a section of Mizo reached back the Khampat area in the beginning of the 20th century the branches then just reached the ground, and they were warmly welcomed back by the headman U Po Theik.

From the light of the above discussions we will now focuss our attention to the different factors which required the Mizo Group to migrate back to Mizoram in India. Some factors may thus be discussed as follows.

Political Development in Mizoram

Following the end of the Second World War, the District authority in Mizoram permitted the Mizo leaders to form a political party. Accordingly, the Mizo Union Party was founded on 9th April, 1946[15]. This new political development thus affected the political life of the people in various ways. But, there soon arose differences of opinion among the political leaders on the future status of Mizoram. These differences then finally led a section of the leaders to form a separate faction in the party known as the 'Mizo Union Right Wing'[16]. This faction staunchly and openly supported the idea of 'Independence' for the people of Mizoram. MacDonald, the then Superintendent, himself secretly supported the group and under his active support the party canvassed all over the district for an independent status of Mizoram[17]. The faction, which supported the 'Independence' thus transformed itself into a separate political party called the United Mizo Freedom Organization (UMFO) on 4th July, 1947. It came into being with the avowed objective of Mizoram joining

Burma. Joined by Lalmawia, a retired army officer in Myanmar, the party, through the influence of Zahrelien, son of the Chief of Falam and a Chin Affairs Council Minister under U Nu, canvassed for joining Chin Hills of Burma rather than remaining in India. Through the interference of Zahrelien, Lalmawia also met Prime Minister U Nu, and discussed the possibility of the Union of Mizoram with Myanmar[18]. His main contention was: the right to secede after 10 years as provided in the constitution of Myanmar and the ethinic closeness of the Mizo with Myanmarese.

This new political development thus taking place in Mizoram, however, had a great repercussion on the Mizo in Chin Hills of Myanmar. They began to realise that their political future was in jeopardy. So, they became panickly and started a sort of movement with a view to consolidating their political status in Myanmar.

The Amendment of Chin Special Division Act, 1957

As noted above, Section 2(4) of Chin Special Division Act was amended in 1957. This amendment then withdrew the citizenship thus awarded to the Mizo. Though restored after the intervention of the Mizo leaders, the action on the part of the government, therefore, kept the majority of the Mizo in the dark and they became suspicious of the government. Thus, many began to develop the idea that one day the government might deport them to Mizoram (India) as foreigners. This idea thus haunted them with fear of deportation. In fact, there were threats of deportations by the government[19]. The assumption came true in the 1974 elections wherein the Mizo were not allowed to contest the elections as citizens of Myanmar. They were, however, allowed to vote[20]. They were allowed to cast their votes only after the insistent appeal by the LWO to the Election Commission. The only antidote to all these problems is the political consciousness among the Mizo. From then on, the Mizo in Myanmar generally did not feel secure and they thus began to return to Mizoram.

The Movement of the Mizo National Front (MNF)

The most important factor which compelled the Mizo to return to Mizoram was the movement of the MNF, the periphery of which was extended beyond the boundary with Myanmar. The Front, founded on 12th October, 1962, raised its demand for 'sovereign independence of Greater Mizoram' and started an armed uprising by declaring 'independence' on 28th February, 1966[21]. As a part of fulfilment to the 'Greater-Mizoram' ideology, political contacts had been made with some Mizo leaders in the Chin Hills of Myanmar before 1966. So, when 'Independence' was declared in 1966, the front leaders declared Chin Hills of Myanmar as their area of operations. Accordingly, strategies were planned to carry out what was known as 'Chin Hills Operation'. Why the Chin Hills of Myanmar was included as part of their operations may be explained as follow :

First, the MNF movement should have an international character.

Secondly, to make it known to the world that the Front leaders wanted all the Mizo occupied areas to come under one administrative unit.

Thirdly, the money or other resources seized from the Chin Hills Operation would be used to meet the expenditures of the contingent to be sent to China to start a political dialogue with the Chinese leaders.

Hence, the MNF volunteers carried out military assaults between May-June, 1968, on military camps at Rihkhawdar, Rih-Camp, Falam, Halkha, Tuibual and Tidim[22]. Except the two operations against Rihkhawdar and Rih Camp, all the other operations were successful. In Tidim alone, they seized more than six lakhs of Kyet which they had utilised for sending the contingent to China.

Consequent upon this, the government then reacted sharply by committing atrocities against the

Mizo in Myanmar. They were suspected and many of them were arrested and put behind bars. Some of them were imprisoned for a number of years[23]. The attitude of the government in particular and the common people in general towards the Mizo was considerably detrimental and they were treated as enemies. So, the way the Government treated them was too harsh to tolerate for some of them. Hence, to escape from the atrocities ravaged by the Government, many began to return to Mizoram.

The Attitude of other Hill People towards the Mizo

The belligerent attitude of the people of Chin Hills towards the Mizo also contributed for the movement of the latter to Mizoram. While government agencies were intensely working to isolate the Mizo group from the main stream of Myanmar, some sections of the people of Chin Hills too, began to destabilise the Mizo in Myanmar. They began to propagate false propaganda that Mizo did not belong to the Chin hills of Myanmar. The idea first originated from Zahrelien himself. So, the seeds of dissension was sown among the people of Chin Hills by the government by means of some sections of the people. Due to this episode many Mizo began to feel that Myanmar was not the best place for settlement. Hence, they migrated back to Mizoram.

The Government Economic Policy

In 1960s General Ne Win took over the government and he introduced a new form of government known as *'Socialism'*. General Ne Win was the man who encouraged the Mizo to join the army and many were recruited when he came to power.

But due to his policy of 'Socialism' the common people including the Mizo had to udergo economic hardships at all levels. The common people suffered mainly from the following reasons:

First, the government collected paddy from the fields at a low flat rate from the farmers. From these forcible collections the agrarians had to lose a big amount of money. People could hardly tolerate this policy.

Secondly, without warning, the government all of a sudden declared a certain currency unit invalid. Due to this action the people including the common people suffered untold miseries[24].

For these two reasons some Mizo came back to Mizoram.

Besides these, individual families or persons might have isolated problems. For example. Thuamliana now 81
(21-2-2002) had his own problem. He was enlisted in

the Persian-Iraq Force with its headquarters in the Middle East. After leaving the Service, he joined his elder brother who was working as a Pastor in Myanmar in 1957 and he returned to Mizoram in 1965. While he was in Myanmar he had a Printing Press and he reprinted some school text books used in Mizoram. These books were taught in the school as text books and this in turn spread the Mizo dialect enormously. But this was very much disliked by some sections of the people and Zahrelien was the main opponent. Because of such minor problems Thuamliana and his family decided to migrate back to Mizoram.

The Chin Group

As already mentioned earlier, the people of Chin group are the original citizens of Myanmar and they are chiefly found in the Chin Hills of Myanmar. They constitute chiefly the two major tribes of *Paihte* or *Zomi* and *Pawi* or *Lai*. Whereas the former are mainly inhabiting the northern areas of Tiddim and Tawnzang of the Chin Hills, the latter are heavily concentrated in Falam, Halkha and Thantlang areas in the Chin Hills. Here in Mizoram, these two communities, still using the different dialects, are integrated among themselves under the banner called "Network for Women Organization in western

Burma". Its President is Mrs. Kipmen and she is doing business.

Like the Mizo-group, these people entered into Mizoram under various circumstances. In this connection, mention may be made of two major factors : the form of government and the economic policy of the government. These two factors are solely responsible for the displacement of the people of Myanmar. But, it is very difficult to discuss these two as separate entities because they are supplementary to each other. Therefore, in this discussion, the two factors will be dealt as one entity.

As we are all aware, the main aim of the socialist governments in the world is to give the means of producing goods and political power to a collective community. In Myanmar, "Socialism" has been the form of government since the 1960s. Though the system seems to be good, the government has, however, failed to deliver goods to the people. The blatant result is that the people now have lost faith in the government because the people now find it very difficult to get even a square meal a day. According to U Phoni[25], a daily labourer has to earn Kyat 200 a day but he has to pay Kyat 400 for a meal. This means that the labourer could not earn even his daily bread. Under such circumstances, the people have nothing to do but to go to the places where they could get their livelihood. Therefore, those people came here to earn their daily bread by doing whatever work they could get. According to Dimkhanching[26], the people of Chin group here in Mizoram have engaged themselves as weavers, domestic servants, and daily labourers. Some of them are also doing a sort of business.

Meanwhile, it may be noted further that in Myanmar the people of Chin group are adherents of different religious denominations like Methodist, Baptist, Roman Catholic Church etc. but here in Mizoram they do a common worship as one community. This may indicate further that the people give more importance to what is called 'nationalism' than their 'religious faith'. But this idea is slowly moving away from them and many of them are slowly joining the local church in the locality where they settle. Again, the main reason behind doing so is that they now really want to identify themselves as true inhabitants of Mizoram.

The Myanmarese Group

Like the other two groups, the Myanmarese came to Mizoram for the same purpose which compelled the other people of Myanmar to migrate to the different destinations. Here we will not repeat what we have said earlier. But in the fitness of things, it may be good to add a few more lines in this discussion about the political developments in Myanmar since 1988. This political development is the obvious reason which has forced the Myanmarese themselves to scatter to different parts of the world. India is one of the countries which has received many Myanmarese refugees and many of them are still in India.

In Myanmar the present political turmoil began when Aung San Suu Kyi came back to Myanmar in March 1988 while the student protests were on in Yangoon. This was followed by the famous 8th August, 1988, mass uprising in which thousands of people were killed on 8th August, 1988. Then on 26th August, Aung San Suu Kyi addressed a mass rally in Yangoon calling for a democratic government[27]. Following this, the military re-established its power and the state Law and Order Restoration Council was formed and this Council took over the administration on 18th September, 1988[28]. At the same time, the National League for Democracy (NLD) was formed with Aung Sun Suu Kyi as General Secretary. To worsen the situation Aung Sun's mother died and the funeral procession turned into a peaceful protest against the military rule[29]. This was followed by the arrest of student leaders.

When the military Junta assumed state power, it declared that it would immediately perform four major tasks, the fourth being "to hold multi-party democratic general elections". Then on 23rd September, 1988, the Defence Services Chief of Staff announced:

> "We have formed a government with a small group of individuals with many responsibilities to carry out the main function that have to be performed by a government and for the continuance of diplomatic relations, so it is obvious that we have no intention to govern for a long time. We respectfully make this promise to the monks and the people of the nation with sincerity and good faith[30]".

Accordingly, the elections took place on 27th May, 1990, and the world acclaimed the elections 'free and fair'[31]. In these elections, 392 members of NLD were elected but the Parliament was never convened by the military authorities.

Being recipient of the people's mandate the Central Working Committee of NLD repeatedly asked the military Junta to convene the Parliament but without success. The NLD then made an appeal to the people to convene Pyithu Hluttaw (Parliament)[32]. The military regime that had seized power then placed Aung Sun Suu Kyi under house arrest on 20th July, 1994. Following the talks Aung Sun was released from house arrest.

However, thing could not be improved, and the result was that thousands of students and political leaders including political activists fled the country.

This was the beginning of 'Diaspora' of the Myanmarese into different parts of the world.

Conclusion

The people discussed above are all foreigners but they do not receive equal treatment from the society. This is obviously only because of the language being spoken by each category of people. Indeed, while the Mizo Group does not have any serious problem with the local people, the Chin group is, however, commonly labelled as "khawchhak mi" which loosely means "men from the east". Though this derogatory term is applied to them, the native people have accepted them in the society without any hesitation.

In this regard, it may be noted further that the case of the Myanmarese (Burmese) themselves is apparently different from that of the other two groups. The local people hardly accept them as they do the Mizo and the Chin groups. Here also the language plays a key role. In the same way, the Myanmarese do not consider Mizoram as their homeland. They know very well that they will go home as soon as the political and economic conditions of the country permit them. They stay but not settled here.

In spite of all this, the idea that all the lands being occupied by Zo people should come under one administration unit currently propagated by a section of the people plays a very significant role in treating and accepting the people coming from the 'east' on equal footing.

References

1. Statistical Handbook Mizoram, Directorate of Economics & Statistics, Mizoram, Aizawl, 2002, p. viii.
2. No one knows for sure why and when the Mizo called the Myanmarese 'Kawl', Myanmar (Burma), has sometimes been referred to as Kawlvai then Mizo called the English as 'Vai' meaning simply 'non-Mizo'. Kawlvai, may, therefore, mean 'non-Mizo other than the English'. Literally 'Kawl' may mean 'ferocious' 'savage' or 'fierce'. Therefore, it may be conjectured that the Myanmarese were rather ferocious or savage. For further information kindly refer to Rev. Liangkhaia, Mizo Chanchin, Mizo Academy of letters, Aizawl, 1976. (4th Ed.) pp. 11-2.
3. B. Lalthangliana, *History of Mizo in Burma, Zawlbuk Agenices*, Aizawl, 1977., p. 27.
4. Hualngo Literature and Cultural Association (HLCA), Zofate Chanchin, Tahan, 1995, p. 104.
5. Rev. Tuahhranga, *Kawl Rama Mizo Lut Hmasate Chanchin Part-I*, R.D. Press, Aizawl, 1984, p. 1.
6. Ekthawla was also known as Hrangtlira. B. Lalthanglina; op.cit. p. xiii.
7. Rev. Tuahhranga; op.cit. p. 1.
8. Ibid.
9. Thanruma, *Kawlram Leh Kei*; Tahan (n.d. p. 12)
10. Ibid.
11. HLCA; op.cit, pp. 105-106.

12. War Office Council Order No.40/50 of Dated 2nd May, 1950. Adjutant General's Department (No. 5743/1/a-2).
13. B. Lalthangliana, op.cit, p. 49.
14. HLCA : op.cit. p. 107.
15. R.Vanlawma, *Ka Ram leh Kei (My Country and I), Zalen Cabin,* Aizawl, (3rd ed.) 1980, p. 134.
16. Sangkima, *"The Process of Merger of Mizo Hills with India"*. Paper presented in the National Seminar on The Making of the Union held at Assam University, 1998.
17. Animesh Ray, *Mizoram-Dynamic of Change,* Pearl Publishers, Culcutta, 1982, pp. 122-123.
18. B.B. Goswami, *The Mizo Unrest,* Aalekha Publishers, Jaipur, 1979, pp. 136-137.
19. B.Lalthangliana; op.cit., p. 65.
20. Ibid. p. 66.
21. Lalrimawia, *Mizoram History & Culture Identity,* Spectrum Publication, Guwahati, 1995, p. 134.
22. Lalrawnliana, *Zoramin Zalenna A Sual Vol.* 6, R.M. Press, Aizawl, 1999., p. 134.
23. Ibid., pp. 163-207.
24. S.T. Sangvunga, an informer, left Mizoram for Myanmar and was enlisted as sepoy. After serving 5 years he left the army and did some business, came back and returned to Myanmar in 1958. He then returned to Mizoram in 1978. Now, he is 71 years of age. Interview on 21.2.2002.

25. U Phoni, Secretary of Burmese Weavers Association, Mizoram, was interviewed on 13.4.2002. He came to Mizoram in 1979.
26. Dimkhanching, an informer came from Myanmar to Mizoram in 1980. Now she lives at Chaltlang, Aizawl.
27. *"Brief Biography and Background of Aung Sun Suu Kyi"* distributed by NLD Liberated Area (Youth).
28. Ibid.
29. Ibid.
30. Statement No. 82 (10/98) National League for Democracy. No. (97/B) West Shwegondine Road, Bahan, Yangoon.
31. Statement No. 52 (8/98)
32. Statement No. 35 (19.8.98)

6

Impact of Chakma Settlement on Mizoram

O. Rosanga

This study is subject to certain limitations especially for the critical analysis of the topic discussed. First of all a brief historical background of the Chakma infiltration since the British rule will be highlighted. It is an attempt to interpret facts with perspective study. On the whole, some of the political effects and both the social and economic impacts resulting from 'Cross Border' movement will be the basic point fervently referred to in this paper. Further, the ethnic problems existing within the District and outside, and strategic interest of the government of India will be other interesting critical notes in this respect. (Strategic interest of the Government could have been an important point to highlight in this article, but as it needed more source materials, it will not be referred in the present context). The theoretical concepts and approach may permit a great deal of understanding on the topic being expressed in this article. On the whole the argument made is that the Chakma Foreigners who crossed the border and have now settled in India, cannot be property dealt with except by viewing it in a historical perspective. Lastly, as far as possible detailed statistical references will be totally ignored. The population of Mizoram is, with the exception of immigrants like the Chakmas and Riangs, all one race or tribe. The Mizo are mostly Mongoloid stock in origin. The language spoken by the bulk of the population throughout the state is Mizo language. The Chakmas who had recently crossed the border from Bangladesh (formerly East Pakistan) since the early twentieth country are mostly found in the western belts of Mizoram bordering Tripura and Chittagong Hills of Bangladesh. In the Chakma areas we can also find sub-tribes of the Mizo such as Pang, Bawm and Tlanglau who were originally the inhabitants of the present Chakma District, but were forced to succumb to the rule of foreign settlers in their own land. Under the British Imperial rule, the Chakmas started to visit Mizoram occasionally, and later under certain circumstances many of them started to cross the border land to the Western Hills. Gradually, a number of times the Chakmas requested the Mizo chiefs to let them settle in their land (usually to cultivate chief's land to sustain their economy). In fact, since 1898 the Tribal Chiefs were given a specific area or boundary of their rule[1]. As the chief was the symbol of the tribe, with the permission of the authority he could allow certain number of Chakmas to cultivate in his land, on condition that they would pay certain taxes to the

Government, but they were not allowed to stay permanently in the Hills. One such occasion may be mentioned. By November 1919, Liankaia, Chief of Kawilam was permitted by the authority to allow forty families of Chakmas of Rangamati, Bangladesh to settle in his land, but they were not to be separated by distances[2]. Actually, Liankaia was asked by the Chakma foreigners to cultivate in his land[3]. The Government in fact issued a strict order that any person who crossed the border of Mizoram from the Chittagong Hill Treats (District) of Bangladesh were not allowed to cultivate without prior sanction of the chief and the authority[4]. (Such orders were already issued under political order No. 24, 30th November 1915 and were re-enacted for general information). Since 'cross border' movement could not be easily checked, the influx of the Chakmas also increased year-by-year. Thereby, the Registration of Foreigners Act, 1939, which was declared by the Governor in Council, was made effective to the whole of British India[5]. As a consequence of this outcome on 8th April, 1939, the Legislative Department with the assent of the Governor General promulgated for general information Act No. XVI of 1939, an Act to provide for the registration of foreigners in British India. This was published in the Assam Gazette on May 3, 1939, Part VII[6]. Mizoram also followed suit with certain modifications and alteration of the clause No. 91-F. Dated Simla, 15th May, 1939[7].

Though the Registration of Foreigners Act was implemented, the infiltration of Chakmas still increased. Because of this, certain principles were made to be observed in dealing with Chakma Settlement in the South Hills of Mizoram[8].

Now, Chiefs were made responsible for the control of Chakmas in their jurisdiction. But within a few years the influx of Chakma Foreigners became quite significant. It was reported that about twenty seven families of Chakmas and Tripuris migrated to the Hills during 1948-49[9].

In fact the Partition of India had greatly changed the political situation of East Pakistan[10]. It also considerably altered the attitude of the Chakmas living in the Chittagong Hills. As a result, the Chakmas started to cross the border land in swarms seeking a new home in India. It was therefore argued that "allowing further free influx would be seriously detrimental to the interest of the people of this District" (Mizoram)[11]. It was further stated that "If the Chakmas are treated as Non-Lushais they will be liable to pay house tax at the rate of Rs. 5 and also other taxes such as Court and Stamp duties"[12]. Thereby, to check the infiltration of foreigners new passes were issued and any chief who did not report Chakma foreigners was dealt with severely. But a number of Chakmas had infiltrators into Mizoram [13].

It is to be noted that there was no cordial relationship between the Bangladesh Muslims and Chakma Buddhists of Chittagong Hill. Therefore, the Chakmas had an aspiration of how they could remain in their homeland, i.e., Bangladesh. They now seriously considered which country or state would prove the best sanctuary for the Chakma people[14]. They looked towards India, the nearest country as the best asylum for the Chakma people. Hence, when the Government made a decision of announcing the Pawi-Lakher Autonomous Region, the Chakma foreigners were stirred by such development. Gradually they started to involve themselves actively in the policies of Mizoram. At any cost they made every move to fulfil their interests, and their objective so far was to have a separate District within the Union Territory of India.

Politically, the Chakmas became quite active soon after the Pawi-Lakher Autonomous Region was inaugurated on 23rd April, 1953 at Lunglei by Ch. Saprawanga, the then Parliament Secretary[15]. This had brought about certain changes in the minds of the Chakmas of both Bangladesh and India. Now the Chakmas of India occasionally made serious complaints and allegation to the Assam Government against the District Council of the Mizo Hills. They stated that it was to safeguard and to fulfil the aspiration of the Chakmas in the Indian soil. To take more active part already in 1953 they had organised a 'Chakma National Sathdin (freedom) Party'[16]. The aim was to have an organised "Regional Council" for Chakmas in Mizoram. This could have been the most serious political implication undertaken by a foreign subject since British rule. By this time the Chakmas living close to the border were also making active arrangements to fight against the Muslim domination[17]. To pursue the matter they further submitted a memorandum to the government demanding a Separate Chakma Regional Council[18]. But it was not seriously meritted on the ground that the number of Chakmas was very small. Therefore, the Chakmas of India started encouraging Pakistani (Bangladeshi) Chakmas to cross the border in swarms to gain more population especially in the Mizo Districts.

> "...the real motive behind the scene was to increase their population and later a 'Regional Council' followed by 'Autonomous District' and finally to gain Independent territory for the Chakmas and even to accommodate their brothers living outside the District Mizoram to free themselves form the Muslim domination"[19].

Prior to this, from June 1952 most of the Chakmas got voting rights and even cast their votes in the first Mizo District Council Election, and this was retained till date.

While the political atmosphere of Mizoram, not yet fully developed, was as its crucial stage, Mizo Independent Movement started in 1966. Taking advantage of this trouble, the Chakmas clandestinately made effort to gain political advantage in Mizoram. Finally by 1972 under the so called 6th Schedule of the Constitution of India, the Chakmas were given a separate Autonomous District Council.

The first and immediate impact as a result of "Cross Border" movements made by the Chakma people was the ethnic problem in Mizoram. As the infiltration of the Chakma increased, the sub-tribes of the Mizo of the western belt such as Pang, Bawm and Tianglau began to lose their ancestral land. Under the Chakma District they had no significant share in the district administration. Moreover, there was no cordial relation between the Chakmas and their neighbouring districts. A small section of the Mizo tribes who were in the Chakma district were denied any prosperity, instead they were now pushed to the corner by the so called 'permanent immigrants' of India. On the other hand, the Mizo themselves could not reach concensus at par with the Chakmas. Further, the Chakmas always showed their willingness to ignore the Mizo language. It is said that "The Chakma District Council does not give any grants, in cash or in kind, to the school where Mizo is used for the medium of instruction"[20]. It therefore implies that the Chakmas did not really regard themselves as part and parcel of the Indian Nation. In spite of abundant sympathy to them by the Central Government, the Mizoram State experienced some small scale communal conflicts, and the communal differences always became the main issue involved in the ethnic problem. Hence, this had become a serious problem for both the Chakmas and the rest of the Mizo Tribe. Thereby, "cross-border" movement signifies an experience to 'Communal disharmony' in the state.

Right from the beginning the Chakma immigrants were aware of their erstwhile status in India. At the initial state, their intention was to be in "Political Good Book" of India, and to have "Free Chakma Zone" in Mizoram[21]. Gradually, the Chakmas could have "Territorial Asylum" by occupying 686.35 Sq. Km. of land in India (in Mizoram)[22]. The impact of Chakma settlement in Mizoram was much more evident when they gained Political Status in India. In almost every Mizoram Election they usually have had two members to the Legislative Assembly (from their District alone).

Through political privileges, the Chakmas could now look forward to their future action plan–Union Territory and later Chakma Independent country at the expense of Mizoram and Tripura, and the Nation as a whole. They now convinced the other two districts Lia and Mara Autonomous Districts into demanding a separate Union Territory for the Chimtuipui District (this will need further research work). It is stated that "the more surprising case is that the leaders of the Chakmas are pressing the Central Leaders of the Indian Union to extend their district with the inclusions of Truipuibari, Marpara and Sazaikawn at the expense of Mizoram[23]. This shows that the Chakmas already had made their best efforts to extend their area, even beyond India. Every effort was made to win the favour of the Central Government. On the other hand, directly or indirectly Mizoram State had become the victim and was forced to consider the Chakma problem under the 'dictated' authority of the Central Government. Hence the consequences of 'Cross Border' movement became significant in a negative form. The impact of the influx of the Chakmas further increased the population of the State and the Nation. Since the inception of the Chakma District their population rose tremendously. Let us now look at the Chakma population between 1901-1991 with percentage of growth[24].

By looking at the Statistical reports, the Chakma population rose tremendously. If one looks at the population based on the nation's economy the share of the Chakmas could have increased year by year. By 2000-2001 under the Non-Plan (for the Chhimtuipui District) the budget spent under different heads or actual expenditure was Rs. 2612.89 lakh. Out of this the Chakma District alone spent Rs. 540.55 lakhs[25]. By 2001-2002 the total Revised Budget Estimate was Rs.

3024,90 lakhs, and the Chakma District spent Rs. 608.406 lakhs[26]. And for the year 2002-2003 the Non–Plan Budget Estimate was Rs. 3108.00 lakhs, and the Chakma's share will be Rs. 625 lakhs[27]. Moreover, in the actual plan for the year 2002-2003, the plan estimates for the Chhimtuipui District was Rs. 1819 lakhs and the Chakma District Council Budget estimates was Rs. 455 lakhs[28]. Not to mention the past fifteen years or so, the total capital involved on the Chakmas (for both the Plan and Non–Plan within 2000-2003 alone) was Rs. 2088.95 lakhs. The Budgets are usually made to sustain a specific population, but once the number increased the amount of budget estimated submitted to the State Government or to the Central Government could have been very high. It therefore implies that due to the infix of the Chakmas the Budget Estimates of the State as well as the Central Government increased. While many Indian families or poorer section of the society could not even get their daily subsistence, the so called immigrants' devoured the nation's economy, or otherwise drained the wealth of India. Hence, "Cross Border" did not have any positive significant result, but had a negative impact on the State economy.

The social implication is another important result that can be seen as a consequence of 'Border Crossing'. Socially the Chakmas hardly involved themselves in the social activities of Mizoram. They kept themselves apart form the main social norms and obligation of the Mizo Society or Indian Society. By alienating themselves from the mainstream of the society they also ignored any social contribution to the State. Even the largest Non-Government Organisation like the Young Mizo Association could not extend its influence in the Chakma inhabited areas. Apart form this, Students Association like the Mizo Zirlai Pawl could not bring any positive results in the Chakma District. Since the early days of their inroads into Mizoram border areas, and their subsequent settlement till date the Chakmas hardly had any consideration to the social norms at par with the people of Mizoram of India. The most serious thing is that they would not adapt themselves to the Mizo Culture. While alienating themselves from the mainstream of the society they at the same time had indirectly shown 'non-cooperation' to the Mizo Society. Therefore, the social impact felt was isolation with communal offences to the State. On the other hand, because of certain political pressure and social obligation 'son of the soil' could not enjoy any freedom of movement or to settle in the inhabited Chakma District. One way or the other, they made themselves hardly accessible to others especially the Mizo. For these reasons the rightful owners of the country could not always utilise the natural resources of their land. Hence the Chakma settlement in Mizoram resulted in 'land alienation' and 'communal disharmony' showing its ugly head to the traditional institutions of its people. The United Nations Charter states that, "sphere of the right of peoples and nations to permanent sovereignty over their natural wealth is a question which comes within the overall field of human rights"[29].

In fact, the Chakma influx and their settlement could have been a mere state problem, but it was deliberately made an international issue. Internationally the moral character and sentiment of the people of the state were hit hard by selfish motives, trickery and alleged designs. Thereby, the people of Mizoram experienced moral degradation. Memorandum and false propaganda were the day-to-day experience during the past years, perhaps even today. The reverse impact could have been avoided had the 'immigrants' been satisfied with what they were already awarded by the Government, i.e., a separate District. Hence, the influx of the Chakmas and their subsequent settlement in India and not only an immediate impact on the community, but far reaching consequences, which were quite disastrous as well as harmful and detrimental to the affected State and its people.

References

1. O.Rosanga, *"The economic History of Mizoram for 1900-1940"* Unpublished Thesis, Chapter I.Part II - Administrative Changes, p. 38.
2. *Reply to Linakais's letter, Chief of Kawilam,* Aijal, 22nd November 1919. Superintendent, Lushia Hill (Government of Mizoram).
3. File A. 1919-20. Pass No. III 1919-20. Letter, Superintendent, Lushai Hills; from Liankaia, Chief of Kawilam, dated 20.11.1919 (Government of Mizoram).
4. Ibid.
5. Registration of Foreigners (Exemption) Order, 1939.No.21/32/39/ Pol. Dated 21 June, 1939 (Government of Mizoram).
6. Government of India, Legislative Department. Secretary to the Government of India Act No. XVI of 1939, 8 April, 1939 (Government of India).
7. Memo No. 173/5 Aijal, the 18th July, 1939 (Government of India).`
8. Memo No. 173/D/C III-19 Lungled, the 22nd March 1944. Chakma settlement in South Lushai Hill (Government of Mizoram).
9. Superintendent Lushai Hill 20.8.1949. Through Lushai Clerk (Government of Mizoram).

10. Chawagkunga C., *Chakma Settlement in Mizoram,* 1983, For detail see pp. 6-31.

11. Memo No.II-7/50/65-8; Letter, Secretary to the Government of Assam Tribal Areas, Shillong, from Superintendent, Lushai Hills Aijal 11th Oct. 1950 (Government of Mizoram).

12. Ibid.

13. Memo No. LGP. 11/53/26, Lungled, the 17th August, 1953 (No. 7833 G.G.P.5/53, 25-8-53) Lushai Hills (Government of India).

14. Weekly confidential Report of Lungled Sub-Division for the week ending the 19-9-1953. p. 3. (Government of Mizoram).

15. Forthnightly Confidential Report of Lungle Sub-Division for the Forthnight Ending the 25th April, 1953. (Government of Mizoram).

16. Weekly Confidential Reports of Lungled Sub-Division for the week ending the 12th December, 1953 (Government of Mizoram).

17. Weekly Confidential Report of Lungled sub-division for the Week Ending the 16th January, 1954 (Government of Mizoram).

18. Copy of Letter No.E/10616/C-10, Aijal, the 4th December, 1954, Also see Memo. No. RCL/4/55/170 dated Lungle, 11th April, 1955 (Government of Mizoram).

19. O.Rosanga, "*Three Economic Conditions and The Social Consequences As A Result Of The Emergence Of The Pawi-Lakher Autonomous Region*". Historical Journal Mizoram.

20. Chawngkunga C., op.cit. pp. 30-31.

21. *Chakma Influx* by Students Conference for Action Programme, Aizawl, dated 20.4.1983.

22. Statistical Handbook, Mizoram, 2000. Directorate of Economics & Statistics, Government of Mizoram. p. XI.

23. Chawngkunga C., op.cit.p.31. See also, *Mizoram Boundary Affairs Including Chakma Case.*

24. Statistical handbook, 2000; op.cit. p. XI.

25. Demand for grants, 2002-2003, Government of Mizoram, Demand No. 27, District Council, p. 120.

26. Ibid.

27. Ibid.

28. Ibid.

29. G.S.Bajwa, *Human Rights in India; Implementation and Violations,* Anmol Publications, New Delhi, Reprint, 1997. p. 68.

7

Impact of Myanmarese Settlement

F. Lalremsiama

Before the advent of the British and the introduction of their administration in the Hills of western Burma and Mizoram, there was no clear cut demarcation of boundaries between the various territories held by different tribes. Inter-tribal feuds and warfare were constant features among them. Might was right and the right to occupation and subjugation of the subdued usually led to transfer of territory to the victors. During the heyday of the Pawi (Lai) tribes of the Chin Hills (till the third quarter of the nineteenth century) the area of their suzerainty extended from the Chindwin river in the east, the Tlawng river in the west, the Bay of Bengal in the south and Southern Manipur in the north. In fact, they regarded all the tribes of Assam-Chittagong Hill Tracts as tribute bearers. This is clearly indicated by the fact that they even collected taxes from the Sailo chiefs who lived as far west as the Tlawng river.

But the resurgence of Sailo (a ruling family of the Lusei tribe) in the middle of the 19th century altered the course of their history. They, with the help of the Fanai tribe in the Southeast, were able to completely check the westward incursion of the Pawi tribe. Therefore, by the time of the advent of the British, Tiau river served more or less as a boundary between the Pawis and the Lusei-Fanai tribes. Ethnologically, the tribes of the Chin Hills of Burma and Mizoram and Southern Manipur of India are related. Though a particular tribe could claim majority in their territory, a fair amount of other tribes would also reside in their midst. Such was the case in terms of ethnic distribution even before each tribe had been confined within a particular area.

Then came the British and their administrative system, in the last quarter of the 19th century, dividing the tracts according to their own administrative convenience, and this created a devastating impact upon the people. The problems it created appear to have far reaching consequences and its divisiveness irrevocable. The Zo ethnic groups of India, Burma and Bangladesh, numbering in millions[1], who could have been reckoned with as a formidable nation if undispersed, have therefore, been dispersed and minimised. They are now termed as minorities in each country that they adhere to, embracing anything, any system, whether social or political, with or without their consent. The people of Mizoram are better off in various aspects while their counterparts in Burma face a number of problems with respect to economic and political matters. These problems are responsible for the cross border immigration of tribes from Burma into Mizoram. In the constitution of the Union of Burma, drafted in 1947, General Aung San promised the non-Burman equality and autonomy. After the death of Aung San, however, U Nu and the AFPEL amended the draft constitution betraying both the letter and the spirit of the Panglong agreement. The amendments invalidated the recognition of the proud nations of Arakan, Chin, Kochin, Karen, Karenni, Mon, and Shan. Therefore, serious trouble was looming on the horizon for Burma at its independence in 1948[1].

Shortly after the independence of Burma, the Karens started an armed rebellion for independence which was followed by several other non-Burman nationalities.

The Burmese government attempted to crush the rebellions with utmost severity resulting in the exodus of the people of Chin Hills into Mizoram. The Burmese government failed miserably in their aim of achieving a socialist state. It was just a utopian dream. Mismanagement of economy, corruption and lust for power disrupted everything. The morale of the common people remained very low. Of course the military government, the all powerful administrative machinery was able to exact necessary requirements such as labour and taxes from the people for running the country somehow. Yet, no significant development has been achieved in any field. For years Burma has remained among the poorest nations of the world. Although she has the potential in terms of raw materials to elevate her position, mismanagement and misappropriation of national wealth has hindered her progress towards development. Those who suffer most under this are the proletariat who have nothing to hang on to. Their poverty and hunger has forced them to move to somewhere else in search of better living and security. This rightly applies to the case of most Myanmarese who migrated into Mizoram in search of employment.

As freedom of movement had never been restricted from the time of separation of Burma and India in 1947, there was a period of time when there was a huge Lushai exodus from India to Burma. During the course of three years alone, i.e., 1948-50, more than a hundred families migrated to Burma. Furthermore, as far as could be ascertained, two hundred and sixteen youths were enlisted into the Burmee Army[2]. Besides easy recruitment and better pay prospects in the Burmese army; availability of land in upper Chindwin area or Burma for wet-rice cultivation in contrast with the hard labour and difficulties involved in jhum cultivation in the Lushai Hills District (Mizoram) in India, attracted the

Lushais to Burma. Other attractions were racial affinity between the Lushais and tribals of Chindwin and encouragement given by the Burmee government to such migration by giving liberal rehabilitation loans and making acquisition of Burmese citizenship easy under the Burmese Constitution Art.II(1)[3]. However, since the 60s of the last century, the descendants of the immigrant Mizo and the immigrants themselves did not find favour with the native people. The result was the return of the Mizo from Burma, causing anxiety to a certain extent on the minds of the Mizo of Mizoram. This is because they believed that the people who came over from Burma, brought along with them, a lot of social evils.

Myanmarese immigration can be said to have a positive as well as negative impact on various aspects of Mizo society. One important contribution of the Myanmarese immigrants is in the field of music and fine arts. Talented musicians and pop-singers were among those who crossed over to Mizoram. The young people of Mizoram received them with great enthusiasm in the eighties of the last century. The styles and sounds of these artists had a profound effect on the musical standard of the Mizo youth. Another important positive aspect of the immigration of Myanmarese was their contribution in the field of painting. Although the Mizo people had practised music, painting and other fine arts from olden days, it hardly occupied an important place in the society, particularly after the Christianisation of the people. The old cultural practices of the pre-Christian era had almost vanished into oblivion. Its revival came with the establishment of the Department of Art and Culture which revived and imported from the Chin Hills various Zo dances like Sarlamkai, Chawngiazawn, Paikawnglam, etc., and popularised by the Department. This was made possible, at least to some extent, with the help of the immigrants. Their contribution in this field is commendable.

There is also a small community of educated employed Myanmarese in Mizoram. Most of them are employed in the Department of Education. Their contribution in Science and Mathematics subjects in the Middle and High School level is worth mentioning. According to Sianga of Chanmari, there are more than a hundred Myanmarese employed in the government sector and around fifty in the private sector. Although it may seem absurd to welcome foreigners from the context of employment, which is one of the most serious problems in the countries, importing of specialists in the fields of science, technology and education is a totally different matter. The contribution of the Myanmarese in the field of Science and Mathematics in Mizoram cannot be under-estimated.

On the other hand, the immigration of foreigners from Myanmar has its negative impacts on the social and economic life of the people of Mizoram. About 10%-15% of hawkers and vendors within Aizawl city are constituted by Myanmarese immigrants. More than a hundred shops of almost all varieties including motor vehicle repairing workshops are owned and run by them. Foreign goods like household utensils, clothing, edibles, electronic appliances, etc., are stored, distributed and sold by smugglers from across the border. Therefore, a huge amount of Indian rupees flows out of India to Burma through this channel each day of the year.

A rough estimate can be made regarding the number of illegal immigrants in Aizawl city. This estimate is made from Sunday School attendance in a number of churches and denominations which have been established by the Myanmarese. The total number of attendance in these churches put together ranges from 2200-2500. The exact figures indicate the number of Myanmarese, who have no relatives here in Mizoram. Most of the immigrants of Lusei origin with relatives in Mizoram have been assimilated into the mainstream of Mizo society. According to H. Lalrinawma, of Chhinga veng, Aizawl, the total number of Myanmarese residing in the state of Mizoram will not be less than 50000, at any given time.

The rise of criminal activities such as, theft, robbery, burglary, drug abuse and murder, are attributed by some people to the Myanmarese. Other people put the blame on the insurgency which started in 1966, and which wrought economic distress and social and political upheavals in the State. The other group of respondents said that Myanmarese involvement and responsibility in drug abuse is minimal as most of these cheap drugs like proxivon find their way into Mizoram from Silchar via Vairengte and not from Myanmar. Drugs like heroin which come from Myanmar, they say, are not consumed in large quantities and the demand is less and therefore Mizoram only serves as a route of trafficking. However, herein abuse is a vice that has been disturbing well-to-do families in Aizawl city and other large towns for many years now. According to CID (Crime) reports for the year 1996-2001, the total criminal cases involving IPC and non-IPC (Crime, including MLTP Act) were 1985[3]. Myanmarese nationals were involved in 213 of these cases. Of the 876 cases under ND and PS Act (Excise Deptt.) Myanmarese nationals were involved in 53 cases. These show a high level of criminal involvement on the part of the Myanmarese who constitute only a small fraction of the total population.

The establishment of new churches, i.e., Bethany Baptist Church and Wesleyan Methodist Church in Mizoram by immigrant Myanmarese has created a new landmark in her century old church history. These church denominations had never existed in the

State before. Their establishment created division among the Christians and the search for new members always leaves scars on many of the faithful. The impact of the introduction of new doctrines in a particular religious group is, more often than not, consequential. Recently, the Truth Mission Evangelical Fellowship (TMEF) or Roluminglinana Paw, which originated in Myanmar, was introduced in Mizoram. This met a lot of resistance from some existing denominations such as the Presbyterian and the Baptist Churches of Mizoram. These denominations believe that the new teaching deviated from the true Biblical doctrines. Thus, doctrinal battles have induced and have been waged for some years now. This has left deep wounds on various local churches and has led to the ex-communication of some of the followers of the teachings from the Presbyterian Churches.

Being situated on an international border always has its advantages and disadvantages. Mizoram too has been greatly influenced by its position on the international border. If its cultural, social, political and economic structure is strong enough to withstand negative pressure from across the border, Mizoram, as a State, has a lot to gain from its proximity to Myanmar. But on the other hand, international borders which are too easily criss-crossed without proper papers can pose security problems for the country as a whole in the future years to come.

References

1. Vum Son; "Chin National Day", Golden Jubilee Journal, February 1998, p. 191.

2. Memo. No.815/L.C., Aijal, the 4th July, 1951. Memo No. 605/L.C., Lungleh, the 5th June, 1951. Memo No. 710/L.C., Lungleh, the 12th July 1951.

3. Memo. No.I/C-6(4) (R-8/6) 53/49 S.B. Shillong, the 4th August, 1953.

4. Pu Sianga of Chanmari, Aizawl.

5. Information received from the Crime Branch of the C.I.D., Police Deptt., Aizawl, Mizoram.

   According to the Excise Department Records, of the 70 cases registered under N.D. & P.S. during the year 2001. 14 cases were registered against Myanmarese nationals.

List of Contributors

Dr. F. Lianchhinga (b. 1940) who did his studies privately got his Ph.D degree from Gauhati University in 1996. Having a vast experiences in the field of education. Dr. F. Lianchhinga became an Inspector of schools and after retirement from active service he took up a project on Tribal Residential School Scheme sponsored by the Govt. of India. To his credit Dr. F. Lianchhinga has written a number of books both in Mizo and English The Chakmas : Religious Beliefs and Practices (English-1996) is one of them.

Mr. Lianhmingthanga (b. 1949) an M.Sc (Anthropoligy) from Gauhati University joined the Tripura Police Service in 1976 and after serving a number of years joined the Department of Art and Culture, Govt. of Mizoram, as Research Officer in 1980 and promoted to Senior Research Officer in the Tribal Research Institute of the same Department. Material Culture of the Mizo is one of his books.

Dr. J.V. Hluna (b. 1952) an M.A. in History from Gauhati University joined Aizawl College as lecturer in the Department of History in 1975 and then joined Pachhunga University College, a constituent college in

1977. Dr. J.V. Hluna was awarded Ph.D by Gauhati University in 1985 and now he is Head, Department of History and Ethnography, Mizoram University. Dr. J.V. Hluna, has published a number of books and Education and Missionaries in Mizoram (1992) is one of them.

Dr. K.L. Pradhan (b. 1955) an M.A. in History from North Eastern Hill University (NEHU) secured the first rank for which he was awarded a Gold Medal by NEHU in 1979 and joined his M. Phil. programme and continued for his Ph.D. in the same University which he obtained in 1987. Dr. K.L. Pradhan now a Reader in the Department of History in Govt. Aizawl College published his first book entitled - Brian Hodgson at the Kathmandu Residency 1825-1843(2001). Presently, he is doing Post-Doctoral research under Indian Council of Historical Research, New Delhi.

Dr. Sangkima (b. 1952) an M.A. in History got his Ph.D. degree from Gauhati University in 1986. Dr. Sangkima joined Govt. Aizawl College as lecturer in the Department of History and became a Reader in 1991. Urged by his desire to do research in the study of the Mizo. Dr. Sangkima published his first book - Mizos : Society And Social Changes (1992) and his second book entitled Essays In The History Of The Mizo is coming shortly.

Dr. O. Rosanga (b. 1953) an M.A. in the History from Delhi University completed his M. Phil and Ph.D Degrees in 1982 and 1992 respectively from the same University. Dr. O. Rosanga who joined Aizawl West College as lecturer in the Department of History is now a Senior Lecturer. To his credit he has published a number of research papers in various journals.

Mr. F. Lalremsiama (b. 1959) an M.A. in History from NEHU completed his M. Phil in 1985 from the same University and joined Johnson College as lecturer in 1993 and now he is a Senior Lecturer. F. Lalremsiama has written a number of books in Mizo and Milulak Leh Vairun is one of them. As an active member of Mizo History Association F. Lalremsiama contributed a number of research papers in its journal Historical Journal Mizoram.

Index